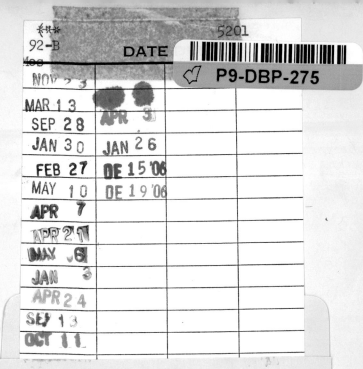

92-Biogr.   5201
Mos

(221.9)   Klagsbrun, Francine

THE STORY OF MOSES

THE STORY OF

MOSES

THE STORY OF

MOSES

by
FRANCINE KLAGSBRUN

FRANKLIN WATTS, INC.
575 Lexington Avenue
New York, N.Y. 10022

Thus the Lord used to speak to Moses face to face, as a man speaks to his friend. Exodus 33:11

Cover photograph courtesy
The Bettmann Archive

Map by Dyno Lowenstein

Note

This book follows the traditional story of Moses as told in the Bible. It is the author's feeling that neither highly fictionalized accounts of the Moses story nor totally realistic, non-miraculous explanations of biblical events are satisfactory means of presenting this powerful saga to young people. The biblical story is a moving and exciting one, and biblical dialogue can be dramatic and poetic enough to grip a young reader's attention. For this reason, none of the dialogue in this book is fictionalized by the author; all is taken from the Bible in the Revised Standard Version translation. To a great extent, also, the author's additions to and elaborations of biblical incidents are based on Christian and Jewish legends and commentaries on the Bible, and on archaeological and historical research.

The following sources were used in the preparation of this book:

The Holy Bible, Revised Standard Version. Cleveland, Ohio: World, 1962.

Albright, W. F. *The Archæology of Palestine*. Baltimore, Md.: Penguin Books, 1951.

Asimov, Isaac. *Words from the Exodus*. Boston: Houghton Mifflin, 1963.

Buber, Martin. *Moses: The Revelation and the Covenant*. New York: Harper, 1958.

Childe, V. Gordon. *What Happened in History*. Baltimore, Md.: Penguin Books, 1964.

Cottrell, Leonard. *Life Under the Pharaohs*. New York: Holt, Rinehart and Winston, 1960.

Davis, A. Powell. *The Ten Commandments*. New York: New American Library (Signet Books), 1956.

Dimont, Max I. *Jews, God, and History*. New York: Simon and Schuster, 1962.

Freud, Sigmund. *Moses and Monotheism*. New York: Alfred A. Knopf, 1939.

Ginzberg, Louis. *Legends of the Bible*. Philadelphia, Pa.: Jewish Publication Society of America, 1956.

Gordon, Cyrus H. *The Ancient Near East*. New York: W. W. Norton, 1965.

Heaton, Eric William. *Everday Life in Old Testament Times*. New York: Charles Scribner's Sons, 1956.

Kraeling, Emil G. *Rand McNally Bible Atlas*. Chicago: Rand McNally, 1956.

Mann, Thomas. *The Tables of the Law*. New York: Alfred A. Knopf, 1945.

Neher, André. *Moses*. London: Longmans, Green, 1959.

Posener, Georges, editor. *Dictionary of Egyptian Civilization*. New York: Tudor, 1959.

Pritchard, James B. *Archaeology of the Old Testament*. Princeton, N.J.: Princeton University Press, 1958.

Wright, George, and Filson, Floyd. *The Westminster Historical Atlas to the Bible*. Philadelphia, Pa.: Westminster Press, 1945.

Contents

FOREWORD

He freed his people from cruel slavery and taught them a new way of life.

He was a man of mystery. And yet he was a man so great that his words and actions still influence the lives of hundreds of thousands of persons.

He lived more than three thousand years ago. But we do not know when he was born or when he died. We do not know where he is buried or what became of his family.

From the beginning he was different. A king ordered that he be killed at birth, but a princess saved him and adopted him as her son. He became powerful and wealthy, but he gave it all up to protect a slave. He was shy and spoke poorly, but he appeared before haughty rulers and made them obey his words.

Because he was a man and not a god, he made many mistakes. Like other men, he felt unhappy and disappointed when things went badly. He sometimes grew angry at his people and at his God. Often, he lost patience with men who did not believe in him. In the end, however, his accomplishments made his failures seem unimportant.

He had only one name. Moses. But that single name was so respected that for hundreds of years his followers hesitated to use it in naming their children.

Tradition says that he wrote the first five books of the Bible. In fact, they are known as the Books of Moses. Almost everything that we know about the life of Moses comes from four of these books—Exodus, Leviticus, Numbers, and Deuteronomy.

The Bible describes many great deeds that Moses performed. He accomplished miracles, such as making water flow from a rock. He defeated powerful peoples, such as the ancient Amalekites. He served as a judge, a warrior, and a statesman.

Most important, Moses gave his people and the world a set of laws and rules of behavior by which to live.

Because the Bible does not give dates, nobody knows the exact dates of Moses' life. Most scholars believe, however, that he lived sometime during the late 1300's B.C. or the early 1200's B.C. Many say that he grew up in Egypt during the time of King Ramses II, who ruled from about 1300 to the 1230's B.C. During this period, great civilizations

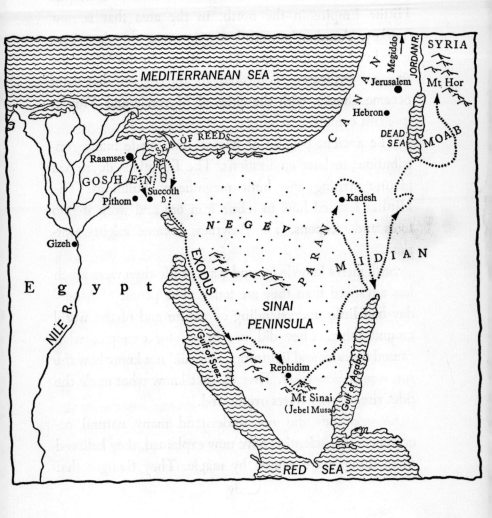

existed in the Near East. Egypt was the wealthiest and most powerful country of the region. Its chief rival was the Hittite Empire in the north, in the area that is now Turkey. Another powerful people were the Assyrians, who lived near the upper Tigris River. In the West, the Aegean civilization flourished in the region that later became Greece, with the cities of Mycenae and Troy as its main centers.

The ancient peoples of Moses' time made many contributions to later civilizations. The Egyptians developed picture writing and built magnificent buildings. The Hittites learned how to refine iron ore and work it into tools and weapons. The Assyrians became mighty warriors.

Still, men's knowledge and ways of life then were much less advanced than they are today. The people of Moses' day had little understanding of nature and of the world around them. They did not know, for example, what caused thunder and lightning. They did not know how the sun rose or how it set. They did not know what made the tides rise, or why rivers overflowed.

Because they did not understand many natural occurrences that scientists have now explained, they believed these things were caused by magic. They thought that there were many gods who made each thing in nature happen. To protect themselves, they worshiped these gods and tried to please them.

People did not expect their gods to be especially good or well behaved. The gods they described had all the faults of human beings. In ancient stories, gods would murder, lie, and steal. They would play tricks on one another and on the people who worshiped them. They were often jealous and cruel.

Most people did not question the actions of their gods. They simply accepted the beliefs that they had been taught and tried not to anger the gods.

Moses was not like most people. He could not accept the idea that there were hundreds, perhaps thousands, of gods ruling the heaven and earth, some looking like animals and behaving like the lowest kinds of human beings. He believed there was only one true God in the universe, greater and better than all the little gods that people had imagined.

Moses set out to teach his people—the Hebrews—about the one God, and to show them new ways of thinking and behaving. To do so, he lived through dangerous adventures, sometimes suffering loneliness and defeat.

During his lifetime, the laws and beliefs that Moses

taught his people made little impression on the rest of the world. The Egyptians went on worshiping their animals and their statues. The people of Palestine went on, as they had for years, sacrificing newborn children to their hungry gods. Even the Hebrews themselves did not accept everything Moses told them. They had lived too long in ignorance and slavery to understand all his teachings.

As time passed, however, and the Hebrews became a powerful people, the laws of Moses became the laws of their land. Gradually, those laws and the ideas that Moses taught, spread to other nations until they came to be accepted in many parts of the world. Today the belief in one God that Moses insisted on forms the basis of almost every religion in the world. And rules of behavior—such as the Ten Commandments—that Moses gave his people are part of the laws of almost every civilized country in the world.

Many things about Moses remain a mystery. Scholars still cannot piece together all the puzzles of his life. Some wonder whether Moses was his real name or whether it is only part of a longer Egyptian name, such as Ptah-Mos or Thut-Mos. Others suggest that some of the Bible stories about him are based on old legends common to many of the peoples of the Near East. Still others question whether

he could possibly have written all the biblical laws himself, or whether many were written after his time.

But none of these mysteries really matter. The story of
Moses' life as told in the Bible is a story of adventure and
excitement. The laws and teachings described there have
come to stand for the most important beliefs that mankind
upholds.

THE STORY OF
MOSES

CHAPTER I

THE SLAVE PEOPLE

As far back as any of them could remember, they had been slaves. They had been born slaves and their children had been born slaves, and most probably their children's children would be born slaves.

They did not question why. They did not even think of ways to change their lives. This is how things were. They could do nothing about it.

But it had not always been that way. They all knew that. Once they had been a free and proud people. Once they had been strong and prosperous. But that was a long time ago. It was so long ago that none of them could imagine what it had been like. All they knew about those times they had learned from the elders of their tribes. And even many of those old men had not been alive during the good days.

But the old tribesmen had much to tell. They knew about things that had happened hundreds, maybe even thousands, of years earlier, almost at the beginning of time. They knew stories that their fathers had told,

3

stories their grandfathers and great grandfathers before them had told.

Sometimes at night, when there was time to rest, the elders would sit among the people and talk to them about the past. Softly, so the guards would not hear, the old men would tell the people about their ancestors, about their God, about how they came to be slaves in the land of Egypt.

They were all descended from a man named Abraham, the elders told them. Like them, Abraham was a Hebrew. He and his family had been shepherds who lived much of their lives in the land of Canaan, east of Egypt.

Abraham and his family had a special God, whom they believed in and worshiped. In fact, Abraham had made a pact with his God, promising never to pray to the gods and statues of other nations, but to worship only Him. In return, God had promised to take care of Abraham's children and all his descendants so that they would grow in number and become strong.

Abraham's son Isaac kept his father's pact with God, and so did Isaac's son Jacob. Because of Jacob's courage and faith, the elders explained, the Hebrews received their other name, Children of Israel. It had happened this way:

One night when Jacob was alone, a man approached him and began to wrestle with him. All night the two

4

men wrestled, until finally, at daybreak, Jacob pinned the man down. Suddenly, Jacob realized that the man was not an ordinary mortal, but an angel of God. Instead of running away or becoming frightened, Jacob held the angel down and refused to let him go until the angel blessed Jacob in God's name. The angel said his blessing and then he gave Jacob a new name, Israel. The name came from two Hebrew words meaning "to wrestle with God." Since that time, all the people who were descended from Jacob were known as Children of Israel, or Israelites.

Many times the elders would also talk to the people about Jacob's son Joseph. Because of him, they said, the Children of Israel now lived in Egypt. But he did not make them slaves. It was just the opposite. Joseph had been a great man, a minister in the royal court.

Joseph was next to the youngest of Jacob's twelve sons, and he was his father's favorite. One day his jealous brothers tied him up and sold him to a caravan of merchants passing through Canaan on their way to Egypt. In Egypt the merchants sold Joseph into slavery. Soon, however, because he was wise and could interpret dreams, the young boy came to the attention of the Pharaoh who ruled Egypt. In a short time, the Pharaoh grew to respect Joseph so much that he made the Hebrew his prime minister.

Joseph did not forget his family after he became rich

and powerful. He forgave his brothers and had them and his father brought to Egypt to live near him in comfort and prosperity. He settled them in the region of Goshen, in northeastern Egypt.

For hundreds of years, the Hebrews who descended from Joseph and his brothers lived happily and peacefully in their land of Goshen. They formed twelve tribes, named for Jacob's twelve sons, and they continued to worship the God of their fathers, Abraham, Isaac, and Jacob.

This was where the elders' stories always stopped. Even they, who knew so much, did not know exactly what happened next to change everything.

All they knew was that somehow, after years of friendship, the Egyptians turned against the Hebrews, as they had turned against other foreign peoples living in their land. Gradually, they forced the Hebrews to work for them, giving them harder and harder tasks and less and less pay, until the Children of Israel became nothing more than slaves, with no rights, no pay, and no relief from their misery.

All day, every day, they worked under a burning sun, mixing mud and straw together to form bricks. Slowly, brick by brick, they built palaces, temples, and storehouses to glorify the name of the Pharaoh.

They saw no way out. They had no hope and no pride.

All they had were their old stories of Abraham, Isaac, and Jacob, and the faded memory of Joseph who had been prime minister of all Egypt.

But what good did those old stories do them at this time, when they were whipped and overworked and spat upon? And where was their God now, the great God whom their fathers had promised to worship? Had He, too, given in to the Egyptians? Had He been beaten by the Egyptian gods the way His people were beaten by their people?

Was there no one to save the Children of Israel?

CHAPTER II

A ROYAL COMMAND

The Pharaoh of Egypt had many names and many titles to honor him. His people called him the Victorious Bull, or Rich in Years, Great of Victories, or He Who Protects Egypt and Subdues the Foreign Lands. There was no end to the names used to glorify his royal highness. Even the name Pharaoh was a special one. It meant "great house," and once had been the term used for the king's palace. Over the years, it had become a title of honor for the king himself.

He was a proud and mighty man, this Pharaoh who ruled all Egypt. He thought of himself as a god, and he dressed in the way he and his people imagined their gods to dress. From his waist hung an animal's tail, a sign of his power over the wildest of beasts. On his head he wore an elaborate headdress that came down low on his forehead. At its center a carved serpent lay poised to strike. People believed that at the Pharaoh's command, the serpent could shoot flames from its mouth to destroy an enemy. At official ceremonies, the Pharaoh tied a false beard around

8

his chin, a symbol of his wisdom and strength. And he carried a scepter, a rod that was supposed to have magical powers.

The empire Pharaoh ruled was one of the most powerful and wealthy in the world. At one time it had been just a small country surrounded by deserts. But the Pharaoh's grandfather and great-grandfathers before him had turned it into a mighty empire that covered hundreds of miles. Egyptian borders stretched far into Asia, into the rich lands of Syria and Palestine. True, in recent years, the Pharaoh had had to send thousands of Egyptian warriors into battle against the Hittites, the Assyrians, and other peoples who had tried to invade his empire. But his armies won many victories and his country remained strong.

People said that his own land, the land of Egypt itself, had been blessed by the gods. Sometimes, as the Pharaoh rode through the countryside in his royal chariot, he would watch the farmers at work on their land. The soil they tilled was rich and black. It was soil that came, as if by magic, from the Nile River that flowed through Egypt. Every spring, after a long, rainless winter when the land became dry and cracked, the Nile would begin to rise and slowly to overflow its banks. Higher and higher the waters rose until they covered almost all the dried lands of the Egyptian farmers. Then, gradually, the waters receded, leaving behind rich earth, perfect for growing barley, wheat, flax, and many kinds of fruits and vegetables.

The thick rich earth was also suitable for making brick and clay with which to build great buildings. Everywhere in Egypt stood beautiful palaces and temples made of the mud-brick that came from Egyptian soil. Many of these buildings had been built by the Pharaoh's ancestors as monuments to themselves. Mostly, they had used gangs of slaves to make the bricks and put up the buildings.

The Pharaoh, too, had set slaves to work building monuments in his honor. Every once in a while he visited the land of Goshen where many slaves were building two great cities for him, the cities of Pithom and Raamses. The slaves who worked in Goshen were different from others in his land. They had not been captured in battle or brought into the country from conquered lands. They were Hebrews, whose ancestors had come to Egypt hundreds of years earlier and had gradually been forced into slavery.

The Hebrews were a dirty lot, with ragged clothes and scrawny bodies. And yet, somehow, they troubled Pharaoh. There were so many of them, and they seemed always to grow in numbers. It was hard to believe that they could go on having families, rearing children, and living long lives under the hardships they suffered. But they did, and their growing numbers worried the Pharaoh.

Of course, it was good to have so many workmen on hand to carry out his wishes. Still, these people were foreigners who hated their Egyptian masters. What would happen if they grew strong enough to join forces with the Hittites or other enemy nations? Could the Egyptians put down an angry army of Hebrew men attacking from within Egypt itself?

From time to time, when the thought occurred to him, Pharaoh planned ways to keep the Hebrew slaves weak and small in number. Once he ordered the overseers who guarded them to increase their work load so that they might collapse from overwork. That plan failed, however. The harder the Hebrews worked, the stronger they seemed to become.

Another time the Pharaoh issued secret orders to the midwives, the women who helped at the births of babies. "When you serve as midwife to the Hebrew women," he told them, "if it is a son, you shall kill him; but if it is a daughter she shall live." That was a good way to weaken the people, he reasoned. Get rid of the men, but let the women live to become house slaves and handmaidens to Egyptian noble families.

But that plan, too, failed, as he might have expected it would. The midwives were too softhearted to kill the

THE STORY OF MOSES

babies whom they had helped to deliver, and they made up all kinds of excuses for not carrying out Pharaoh's orders.

Most recently, the Pharaoh had hit on a new idea. This time he would not depend on some silly sentimental women to destroy the strength of the Hebrews. This time he issued a command to all his people, and it was carried far and wide throughout the land.

"Every son that is born to the Hebrews," Pharaoh commanded, "you shall cast into the Nile, but you shall let every daughter live."

CHAPTER III

Jochebed's Baby

The baby cried and the woman leaned down to quiet
him. He was a lovely baby, round and chubby and happy.
He was three months old, and growing bigger all the time.
And he was smart. He could recognize her voice even
from a distance, and he cooed and smiled at her whenever she spoke to him.

Three months old. Jochebed could hardly believe that
the time had passed so quickly. Yet, every day of those
three months had been filled with fear. Every day she
had awakened in terror, thinking that perhaps this day
would be his last. Every day she had fed him, bathed
him, and hushed him, hoping with little hope that the
God of her people would spare her son one more day of
life.

She remembered those early days after Pharaoh's order
had come. At first nobody could believe it. They could
not believe that the all-powerful Pharaoh of Egypt had
taken it into his heart to destroy the innocent babes of a
slave people. Then, suddenly, Egyptian soldiers were

13

everywhere, and the people knew that the unbelievable was true. Day after day the soldiers came. Behind them they left death, tears, and the stunned silence of parents whose newborn sons had been torn from them.

In her own tribe of Levi, dozens of baby boys had been hurled into the Nile, just as Pharaoh commanded. The Hebrews considered the Levites their priests, and many had turned to them for help. But there was no way of helping. The God of Israel, it seemed, had forgotten His people; nobody could protect them from the cruelty of the Egyptians.

Jochebed herself had been sick with worry. She was expecting a baby when the Pharaoh's command was announced. When the baby came and it was a boy, she had cried out in anger and fear. But she had also made up her mind about one thing: she would not give in the way the others had. She would protect her baby's life as long as she could, even if it meant risking her own life and that of her two older children, Aaron and Miriam.

The moment her son was born Jochebed hid him, not even letting her Hebrew neighbors know that the baby had lived. From then on, her days were spent in keeping him hidden. When the child cried, she quickly lifted him or rocked him. She, or Amram, her husband, or one of their children watched over the little boy constantly, making sure that he was happy and content and that no harm came to him.

But today he was three months old and it was almost impossible to keep the secret any longer. Soon he would be crawling and walking. Surely somebody would see him, and that would be the end, for all of them.

Jochebed had known from the start that a time would come when she could no longer hide her son. She had never wanted to think about that time, and yet all along she had prepared a plan to carry out when the moment did come.

Now she was ready to put her plan into action. Slowly, she took out a little basket that she had woven weeks earlier. She had made the basket out of bulrushes, the heavy reeds that grew along the banks of the Nile. She had covered the reeds with a thick black pitch that becomes firm and hard after it dries. The pitch made the basket waterproof, and that was what Jochebed wanted.

Jochebed placed her beloved son into the little reed basket. She called softly to her daughter Miriam, and together they carried the basket out of their hut, away from the slave quarters, and down to the banks of the Nile. There they placed the basket, with the baby in it, among the tall reeds that grow on the edge of the river.

It was the baby's only chance. Jochebed had often

seen Egyptians strolling along the banks of the river. Perhaps, she reasoned, some kindly person would find her child in his little basket and adopt the boy as his own. She might never see the child again, but at least he would be safe.

For a long while Jochebed stared at her son. Then, quickly, she turned away and walked back to the Hebrew camp. Little Miriam lingered behind. Small and slender, she was able to hide behind the reeds and watch, unseen, over her baby brother.

Time passed slowly for the little girl. Then Miriam heard gay laughter and the chatter of women approaching the bank of the river. As the voices drew closer, she could see the women clearly. One of them was the most beautiful person Miriam had ever seen. She had long black hair and huge eyes outlined in green, the way Miriam had heard that noblewomen painted their eyes. Her dress was made of white linen, long and tight, and around her neck she wore a heavy necklace. Thick bracelets covered her arms, and jeweled rings sparkled on her fingers. The other women wore simpler clothes and seemed to be serving the first woman, whom they addressed as "princess," or "your highness."

Princess? Miriam could hardly believe her ears. Why this was the princess of Egypt, the daughter of the mighty

Pharaoh. And those were her handmaidens accompanying their mistress as she came to bathe in the warm waters of the Nile.

As Miriam watched, the women began to prepare the princess for her bath. All of a sudden the princess stopped and pointed to the little reed basket floating on the water. With a wave of her hand, she sent her maids to fetch the basket and bring it to her. Miriam stood by breathlessly as the princess took the basket and looked inside. Then she saw the princess smile broadly and point to the baby boy, crying now with all his might.

"This is one of the Hebrews' children," Miriam heard the princess say.

There was such warmth and kindness in her voice that Miriam knew immediately that everything would be all right. Pharaoh's daughter was not going to harm the baby at all. In fact, she acted as though she were going to keep him and care for him herself, in spite of her father's command.

Gathering all her courage, Miriam stepped out of her hiding place and said the words that her mother had made her memorize during all the weeks they had prepared their plan.

"Shall I go and call you a nurse from the Hebrew women to nurse the child for you?" Miriam asked. She

17

knew that it was a custom among wealthy Egyptian women to hire nurses to care for their children during their first three years of life.

"Go," answered the princess, and Miriam rushed joyfully away.

A short time later, Miriam returned with Jochebed, never letting on that Jochebed was the boy's real mother.

For a long time the two women spoke together, the Egyptian princess and the Hebrew slave. Finally, when the princess felt convinced that Jochebed would take good care of her newfound son, she handed the baby to the Hebrew woman. Jochebed promised to bring the child back to the princess in three years and the women parted, each going her own way.

Jochebed returned to her cramped slave quarters with mixed feelings. She would have her son with her only a short time longer. After that she would have to give him up forever to Pharaoh's daughter. But she had saved him from death, even from slavery. He would be reared in the court of Egypt as an Egyptian prince. She could not ask for anything more.

CHAPTER IV

PRINCE OF EGYPT

They called him Moses. The princess gave him the name, which meant "to draw out."

"Because I drew him out of the water," she explained when she told people about her adopted son.

Moses heard the story many times. He knew how the princess had found him crying in his little basket in the water and had him brought to the royal palace to be reared as her son. He may have been told that his real parents were Hebrews, but he could barely remember the first three years of his life when he had lived among the slave people. His origins did not trouble him. He was a young prince, growing up in Pharaoh's court. He did not have time to think about people and places of distant days. He had too much to do and to learn.

From early morning until bedtime, Moses' day was filled with activities. First he had classes to attend.

He began classes when he was five years old. While other wealthy boys attended special schools in the capital, little Moses had private lessons in the court. Under the

19

strict care of Pharaoh's priests and wise men, he spent long hours learning how to read and to write.

It was no easy matter to learn the complicated Egyptian writing, and Moses struggled hard with his penmanship. Instead of the letters of the alphabet we use in writing today, the Egyptians used pictures to stand for sounds. A picture of a bee might stand for the sound of "b." A picture of an eye might stand for the sound of "i." A boy had to learn dozens of picture sounds and put them together correctly to form words.

Like other schoolboys, Moses practiced his writing on special scrolls invented by the Egyptians. The scrolls were made of papyrus reeds, the same kinds of reeds that Jochebed had used to make Moses' little basket years before. On his scrolls Moses copied proverbs, stories, and poems, until he could write them clearly and well. For pens he used sharpened reeds, and his ink was made of a mixture of water, soot, and vegetable gum.

The priests watched over everything that Moses did. They seemed to be everywhere in the court. Like the princess and the Pharaoh himself, the young boy came to fear and respect these priests whom people regarded as the servants and messengers of the gods.

From them, Moses learned how to recognize the many gods of Egypt and how to worship them. There were

hundreds of gods to know about—a god of the sun and a
god of the wind, a god of the earth and a god of the sky.
There was a god who watched over people's eyes and ears,
a god who cared for their heads and chests, and a god who
protected their arms and legs. There were gods that looked
like animals and gods that looked like fishes. There were
bird gods, and snake gods, bull gods, cat gods, and croco-
dile gods.

But of all the gods of Egypt, Moses learned, two were
most important. These were Amon-Re, god of the sun,
and Osiris, god of death. Osiris was especially important,
the priests said, because he guarded the Other World,
where people went after they died. From his earliest days,
Moses heard about the Other World in which souls were
supposed to be rewarded or punished for the life they
had lived on earth.

As a member of the royal family, Moses discovered
that he had more of a chance than others of living well
in the Other World after he died. Special tombs had
been designed for Pharaoh and his family to help them
in their life after death. In these tombs workmen placed
food, drink, clothing, jewels, and all kinds of treasures
that people believed would aid the soul on its journey to
the Other World. Craftsmen painted beautiful pictures
on the walls of the tombs, showing how the Pharaoh and

his family had lived on earth, in the hope that they could continue the same good life after death.

Only the rich and noble—like Moses and his adopted family—could afford such elaborate tombs. Poor people could not, and so they had little hope of happiness in the Other World. But in the royal household in which Moses lived, few persons ever thought about the poor. The priests and noblemen told their young charge again and again that the poor were on earth only to serve the rich. They were barely worthy of entering the Other World, except perhaps as servants.

Sometimes on journeys with other members of the royal family, Moses passed through the city of Gizeh, called by his countrymen the City of the Dead. There he could see some of the greatest tombs ever built in Egypt. These were the pyramids, built for pharaohs who lived more than a thousand years before the young boy's lifetime. Long before Moses was born, thieves had broken into the tombs and had stolen many of their treasures. But the buildings still stood—as they stand today—reminders of the power and greatness of the pharaohs of Egypt.

Schoolwork and religion were not the only things that occupied Moses' time while he was growing up. There were many exciting ways for the young prince to amuse himself in the Egyptian court.

Perhaps most exciting were the hunts. As he grew bigger and stronger, young Moses was sometimes allowed to accompany Pharaoh and his servants on a dangerous hippopotamus hunt. The Pharaoh and his party would seek out a big hippopotamus in the marshy waters where it lived. Then the Pharaoh would hurl a harpoon at the hippo, and as the animal grew weaker, he would spear it over and over again. His servants would help the Pharaoh attach a rope to the hippo's neck, and together the men would pull the huge animal to shore, all the while praising the Pharaoh for his strength and courage.

Often after a hunt Pharaoh would give a huge party to celebrate his victory over the wild animal. These parties were happy, noisy affairs with many many courses of food and rounds and rounds of beer, the favorite drink of the Egyptians. Flowers decorated all the tables and an orchestra played sweet music throughout the evening. Most of the women wore long black wigs topped by cones of perfumed oil. As the evening went on, the oil melted, giving the women and the room a lovely fragrance. The party's entertainment almost always included beautiful dancing girls who performed to the music of a lyre or a harp.

Dancing and eating, hunting and studying—the days passed pleasantly for Moses as he grew from childhood into manhood in the court of Egypt. If he ever wondered about his early beginnings, he did not speak about them. To the people around him and even to himself, he was a prince of Egypt. He had everything to look forward to, both in life and in death.

Then, one day, he lost it all.

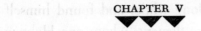

CHAPTER V

THE FUGITIVE

Later, he could hardly remember how it happened.

The day began like any other. He went about his usual activities, saw his friends, spoke with the wise men of the court, and later took a drive in his chariot. Without much thought he entered the slave quarters in Goshen and strolled about, watching the people at work.

He had visited Goshen from time to time, without knowing exactly why he was doing it. Something about these lowly people drew him to them. It was not because they had once been his people—he knew little about that time; they had almost nothing in common. It was just that they seemed to suffer so, and yet their suffering did not defeat them. He felt himself draw strength from their strength as he watched them carry out the hard chores of their lives.

This time, as always, he walked about in silence, looking on as the people shaped their bricks and stacked them into piles, one on top of the other, ready to be used in building.

He walked for a long while, and found himself in a deserted part of the settlement, where one Hebrew man worked alone, sweat streaming down his bare back. Without seeing Moses, the man stopped to rest for a moment. Suddenly, swiftly, an Egyptian overseer appeared. He shouted at the man to get back to work, and with all his might he brought his whip crashing down on the man's back. Over and over the whip lashed into the man while he screamed in pain and humiliation.

Without hesitating, his eyes blazing and his fists clenched, Moses dashed over to the two men, and with one blow, knocked the Egyptian overseer to the ground. Dazed, barely conscious of what he had done, Moses looked down at the overseer, waiting for him to get up and fight back. But the Egyptian did not move. He just lay there, very still, blood trickling from his nose and his mouth.

He was dead. In his burst of fury, Moses, prince of Egypt, had killed an Egyptian officer.

There was no time to think. The Hebrew slave had run off when the fighting began, and Moses was left alone with the dead Egyptian. Quickly, looking from side to side to make sure that nobody saw him, Moses hid the body in the sand and rushed away.

That might have been the end of it. He had acted without thinking, out of pity for a helpless slave. It was over, he had escaped, and he should have behaved as though nothing had happened. But he could not.

The next day he returned to Goshen. Yesterday he had killed for the Hebrews, risking his own life to save one of them. Today he had to speak to them, to be among them, to learn more about them—and perhaps at the same time, to learn about himself and his own beginnings.

Moses walked among the Hebrews, talking to them, looking into their huts, smiling at their children. For the first time he seemed to see them as people, not merely puppets who moved to the command of their taskmasters.

As he was about to leave, Moses saw two Hebrew men fighting with one another. Once again, he acted quickly, and again without hesitating. But this time he did not raise his hand or his voice in anger. He spoke softly, like a father teaching his children.

"Why do you strike your fellow?" he asked the man who had started the fight. To himself he thought: poor beaten people, they do not even know enough to help one another in their misery.

Like a sharp blow, the man's answer struck at Moses.

"Who made you a prince and a judge over us?" he shouted, "Do you mean to kill me as you killed the Egyptian?"

Killed the Egyptian! Moses could hear the thumping of his heart. They had seen him after all. Perhaps this man or another had witnessed the entire incident and had told the Egyptians about it in order to win favors for himself. And why not? What was Moses to the Hebrews? Just another hated Egyptian, no different from the rest. Why should they trust him or protect him?

Without answering, Moses turned away and walked quickly from the camp.

Now he had to act with speed.

"Surely the thing is known," he said half aloud, and the sound of his voice startled him. He was shaking, and his head throbbed as though metalworkers were pounding within it. What had he done and what would he do? Pharaoh's soldiers were probably out looking for him right now. The Pharaoh would have little sympathy. It was not that killing and fighting were unusual among the noblemen of Egypt. But it would be unforgivable for a member of the royal court to kill an Egyptian in order to save a Hebrew slave.

As the thoughts and fears came tumbling out, Moses began to run. Run away, his mind told him, and his legs moved faster and faster. Run away from the Hebrews, those despised, oppressed people he had wanted to help but could not understand. Run away from the Egyptians, the all-powerful, cruel Egyptians he had lived among but did not really belong to. Run away, far away. He must run to find the one person he had never known—himself.

CHAPTER VI

A Lonely Shepherd

The land of Midian lay to the east of Egypt, in the northwestern section of present-day Saudi Arabia. The Midianite tribes who lived in this land were a simple, peace-loving people. Most of them were shepherds who wandered through the dry lands and rocky mountains in search of good grazing grounds for their sheep and goats. Some of the people worked as miners and metalsmiths, traveling to the mountains of the Sinai peninsula, just outside Egypt, to mine copper and turquoise.

The Midianites lived close enough to Egypt to know of Egyptian ways and manners. They were far enough away, however, to be free of Egyptian control, to live their own lives and follow their own customs.

To this land and these people Moses came one afternoon, tired and hungry. He had been running and hiding for weeks, pushing his way through the hot desert sands and empty wildernesses of the Sinai peninsula, always on guard for the Egyptian soldiers he knew must now be searching for him.

Near a well just outside a Midianite village, Moses sat down to rest and refresh himself before continuing on his lonely flight. The water felt good on his dry, cracked lips, and the precious drops of liquid quickly cooled his burning face and eyes.

The well, Moses could see, was a meeting place for shepherds. Groups of them stood around talking and laughing together as they filled their animals' drinking troughs with fresh water. Both men and women brought their flocks to this well, the women gracefully carrying buckets of water away on their heads.

For a long time Moses sat near the well, lost in his own thoughts. But gradually, he became aware of an argument going on nearby. Looking up, he saw a group of young girls gathered around the well, trying to draw water while a band of rough-looking shepherds kept shoving them aside. Moses counted seven girls in the group, all dressed alike in coarsely woven robes, with long shawls wrapped around their heads and shoulders. The girls looked strong and healthy, but not strong enough to fight off the shepherds who spoke gruffly and laughed loudly as the girls struggled to get their water.

Tired as he was, Moses rose and walked over to the group. He cut a strange figure, with his haggard eyes and dirty, worn, Egyptian clothes. But he carried himself with such strength and confidence that the shepherds moved aside as he approached.

Barely raising his voice, Moses ordered the shepherds out of the way. Swiftly and silently, he helped the girls draw heavy buckets of water from the well. While they watered their thirsty flock, Moses kept his eyes on the shepherds, who muttered angrily about the meddlesome foreigner, but did not dare approach Moses or the girls.

When the girls had finished watering all their animals, they thanked Moses and went on their way. As he watched them move along, Moses tried to guess who they might be. Surely they must be sisters, he thought, because of the strong family resemblance among them. Probably they had no brothers, or they would not be out alone tending the flock. Seven daughters! That was a mixed blessing for any man. It meant seven mouths to feed, seven husbands to find, seven dowries to pay. Still, they were pretty girls, especially the one whom they called Zipporah. And they were sturdy. A man could do worse than to have one of them for a wife.

The guessing game was two-sided. All the way home, the girls gossiped busily about the stranger who had rescued them from the shepherds. He was an Egyptian, that much they were sure of. But who? He looked like a nobleman, yet he seemed quite at home watering their animals. What was he doing in their land, and why did he appear so tired and dirty?

By the time they reached home, each girl had made up her own romantic story about the stranger. Each had her own ideas about him and her own daydream about why he had come to help her and the others.

Moses had guessed correctly about the girls. They were sisters who went out every day to tend their father's flock. When they neared their hut, their father heard their voices and came out to greet them.

"How is it that you have come so soon today?" he asked. He knew the difficulties that his daughters had with the shepherds. Often he grieved in his heart for his little girls, burdened with men's work.

"An Egyptian delivered us out of the hand of the shepherds," one of the girls answered, "and even drew water for us and watered the flock."

"And where is he?" the father asked excitedly. It was not often that an Egyptian came to his village—and this one sounded like a good Egyptian. "Why have you left the man? Call him, that he may eat bread."

So the girls went back—not unhappily—to fetch their hero to their father's house. Almost immediately, a friendship sprang up between the two men. Over a meal of bread and goat cheese, they told one another about themselves and their past.

The man's name was Jethro. He was a Midianite priest, not unlike the priests Moses had known in Egypt. Like the Egyptians, Jethro's people worshiped many gods, and he led them in performing rites and services to those gods. For his priestly work the people treated Jethro with great respect. But he was not a rich man in the way that the Egyptian priests were rich. He lived the same simple shepherd life as most of his people.

Jethro listened carefully when Moses told him about himself—about his mysterious beginnings, about the princess and the Pharaoh, about his flight from Egypt. The older man had heard of the Hebrews. He and his people even worshiped the God of the Hebrews along with their own gods.

Before the evening was over, Moses and Jethro had reached an agreement. Moses would stay in Midian and live with Jethro, tending Jethro's flock in return for his living quarters and food.

So Moses settled down to a new life. In place of his smart Egyptian tunic, he now wore a long shepherd's robe, tied around his waist with a thick cord. His elegant Egyptian wigs gave way to a simple turban and wide shawl that protected him from the sun and the wind. His beard, carefully shaven during his years in Egypt, grew long and thick like that of the Midianite men.

His days were hard and lonely. Each morning he set out with Jethro's flock in search of pasturelands for the sheep and goats to feed on. At night, when he and the flock were far from home, he built a tent for himself or slept in a nearby cave. He learned how to build a sheepfold (a wall to enclose his sheep at night), and he trained himself to sleep lightly, alert to any sound of danger to the flock.

In the course of time, Moses married Jethro's daughter Zipporah. He had especially noticed her that first day at the well, and not long afterward had asked her father for her hand in marriage. If Moses' mother Jochebed had known, she might have smiled and told him that he was carrying out a tradition of the Hebrews, for Jacob, one of the Hebrew fathers, had also met and fallen in love with his future wife, Rachel, at a well. Moses and Zipporah lived happily together. When their first son was born, Moses named him Gershom, which came from a word meaning "foreigner." He chose the name because he said, "I have been a sojourner in a foreign land."

As the days wore on, the land of Midian became less and less foreign to Moses. Now it was Egypt that faded

35

into the distance, seeming more like a dreamland than a real place in which Moses had lived. He could scarcely remember the princely life he had led there—the hunts and the chariot races and the big, noisy beer parties.

The only contact that Moses had with Egypt came from messengers and travelers who passed through Midian from time to time. From them Moses learned that the Pharaoh he knew had died and that the Pharaoh's son had taken his place. The new Pharaoh, people said, was even more cruel to foreigners than the former one had been. When Moses heard this, his heart ached for the Hebrew slaves he had known only briefly. But he could see no way to help them.

Alone with his flock hour after hour and day after day, Moses turned his thoughts increasingly inward. He wondered about the strange events of his life that had led him to this place and this way of living. Was he destined now to spend the rest of his days here, working as a simple shepherd? Or did the gods he had heard so much about have still more in store for him?

CHAPTER VII

A Fire That Did Not Burn

"Moses!"

The earth seemed to shake with the sound of his name.

"Moses!"

Again he heard it, louder than before, the same voice calling his name out of nowhere—and everywhere.

"Here am I," he whispered, looking around to see who was calling him. There was no one, just emptiness for miles and miles.

I must be dreaming, he thought. This could not be real. But even as he thought it, he knew that he was fooling himself. He was as awake as he had ever been, his senses clear and alert to the sights and sounds about him.

He looked again at the bush. That was what had attracted him here in the first place. He had wandered far with his flock that morning, westward to the edge of the wilderness, where mountains rose to the sky and tangled bushes seemed to grow one on top of the other.

He had found himself near the mountain that people called Mount Horeb or Mount Sinai. Jethro often spoke

37

of that mountain as a holy spot, where strange events took place. Sensing that he had gone too far, Moses had begun to herd his flock back when a flicker of red at the base of the mountain caught his eye. Fire! he had thought, and had rushed over to push his sheep and goats out of the way.

Then he had seen it, this blazing bush whose flames danced up at him even now. It was the strangest sight he had ever seen. The fire burned deep within the bush, yet not a single branch was charred, not a leaf blackened with smoke. The fire blazed on and on, but the bush was not burned.

As Moses stared at the flames, he heard the voice again.

"Do not come near," the voice said, "put off your shoes from your feet, for the place on which you are standing is holy ground."

Stiffly, almost in a trance, Moses obeyed the voice. Quickly he slipped his sandals off his feet in the sign of respect he had seen many times in the temples of Egypt and Midian.

And now the voice went on.

"I am the God of your father, the God of Abraham, the God of Isaac, and the God of Jacob," it said, and the sounds seemed to swirl around him.

Terrified, Moses hid his face in his arms. But he

38

did not move from the spot on which he was standing.

"I have seen the affliction of my people who are in Egypt," the voice continued, "and have heard their cry because of their taskmasters."

The words pierced Moses' mind and heart. "God of your father . . ." ". . . my people who are in Egypt . . ." Somewhere within him a memory stirred, a memory he could not quite grasp. He had heard those words before. Long ago, in a little mud hut he had heard about the God of the fathers, the God of Abraham, Isaac, and Jacob, who would come to save His people from the cruelty of the Egyptians. He had heard it but he had forgotten it. Then the memory faded, and his whole being shook with the sound of the voice.

"I know their sufferings," the voice continued, "and I have come down to deliver them out of the hand of the Egyptians, and to bring them up out of that land to a good and broad land, a land flowing with milk and honey, to the place of the Canaanites, the Hittites, the Amorites."

His head was bursting and he could hardly breathe. The Canaanites, the Hittites, the Amorites—Moses knew those names well. They were nations of Asia with whom the Egyptians had fought. He had followed the battles carefully in his days at court. A land flowing with milk and honey—that would be a rich land, where people could have as much to eat as they wished. What was this voice telling him? That the ragged, beaten slave people would fight the powerful nations of the world and win themselves a rich land of milk and honey? How was that possible?

As though hearing his thoughts, the voice said, softly, almost tenderly, "Come, I will send you to Pharaoh that you may bring forth my people, the sons of Israel, out of Egypt."

There was a stillness in the air now as the words burned their way into Moses' mind. "I will send you to Pharaoh . . ." You, Moses. You, child of the slave people. You, murderer of the Egyptian. You, shepherd of Midian. In a second, his whole life flashed before him and he knew what he had never known before. He knew why he had been spared in his little reed basket while other babies had been destroyed. He knew why he had killed the Egyptian overseer and why he had lived the long, lonely years in Midian among the priest Jethro and his people. He knew, without being told, that all the events of his life had led up to this one moment, the moment he was chosen by God to free His people.

He knew, but still he did not understand.

For the first time, he dared to speak, and his words came haltingly.

"Who am I that I should go to Pharaoh, and bring the sons of Israel out of Egypt?" he asked softly.

The answer he received was simple.

"I will be with you," the voice answered. Nothing else mattered.

For a long time there was silence, and it seemed to Moses that he was alone in the world. The trees and mountains, the sheep, the land seemed flat and far away now, as though they were painted on canvas. The only thing that was real was the voice coming from the flaming bush.

After a while the voice of God began to speak again. In great detail, Moses learned how he was to carry out his mission. First, he was to gather the elders of Israel and tell them all that he had seen and heard. Then together they were to go to the Pharaoh of Egypt and ask permission to take all the Hebrews into the wilderness for three days so that they might "sacrifice to the Lord our God." The Pharaoh would refuse, God told Moses, and then God would save Moses and His people and perform great deeds to show the Egyptians His might.

Moses listened carefully, calmer now than he had been. But inside he was troubled and filled with doubt. He wanted to believe—he did believe—in this voice and this invisible God who was the God of his fathers. But he had been asked to do more than believe. He had been asked to speak to others, to make them accept what he had seen, and to convince them to follow him as he obeyed the commands of his God. That was no easy task. Even the elders would think him a madman to talk to them about a land of milk and honey when they barely had a piece of bread to chew on or water to quench their thirst.

Hesitatingly at first, then more boldly, Moses began to question the voice in the burning bush.

First he wanted to know God's name.

"If I come to the people of Israel and say to them, 'The God of your fathers has sent me to you,' and they ask me, 'What is his name?' what shall I say to them?" he asked.

The answer was no answer, but a puzzle.

"I AM WHO I AM," the voice replied. "Say to the people of Israel, 'I AM has sent me to you.'"

Later, much later, back in this wilderness, near this same mountain, with his bands of Israelites behind him, Moses would finally understand those mysterious words. Right now, however, he could feel disappointment spread through his body. What kind of an answer was that? Why must this God speak to him in riddles when he wanted facts, information he could tell the elders? All the Egyptian gods had names. Surely the people would want to know the name of the God who had spoken to Moses.

Almost angrily, forgetting his fear, he cried out, "They will not believe me or listen to my voice, for they will say, 'The Lord did not appear to you.'" Don't you see, he wanted to say, they are a simple people, these people of yours. They must have proof, something real that they can understand.

Again, the God in the bush seemed to read his thoughts.

"What is that in your hand?" the voice thundered.

"A rod," Moses answered.

"Cast it on the ground."

Obediently, Moses threw his shepherd's staff to the ground. Before he could step aside, the rod turned into a hissing snake, ready to strike at him.

Moses jumped back, and as he did so he heard the voice of God say, "Put out your hand, and take it by the tail."

Gingerly, Moses reached out and grabbed the snake by its tail, only to have it become a rod again in his hand.

Standing there, looking at the rod, he heard the voice speak to him once more.

"Put your hand into your bosom," it said, and Moses tucked his hand under the folds of his robe. When he took his hand out, it was shriveled and white as snow, the way the hand of a man suffering from leprosy might look.

43

Shaken, Moses thrust his hand back under his robe. This time when he took it out, it was healthy and whole again.

Slowly, overwhelmed by the miracles he had just seen, Moses knelt before the flickering flame, bowing his head close to the ground. Around him he heard the voice of God.

"If they will not believe you, or heed the first sign," the voice said, "they may believe the latter sign. If they will not believe even these two signs or heed your voice, you shall take some water from the Nile and pour it upon the dry ground; and the water which you shall take from the Nile will become blood upon the dry ground."

Moses felt weak now, weak and small before the might of this fearsome God who had sought him out.

"Oh my Lord," he said humbly, "I am not eloquent . . . I am slow of speech and of tongue."

"Who has made man's mouth?" the mighty voice interrupted him. "Who makes him dumb, or deaf, or seeing, or blind? Is it not I, the Lord? Now therefore go, and I will . . . teach you what you shall speak."

But still Moses held back. How could he ever express to others the mysteries and wonders of what he had just seen? He was a man of action, not an orator or a statesman. He had a slight lisp and had never spoken in public, not even when he was at the royal court of Egypt.

"Oh, my Lord," he pleaded, "send, I pray, some other person."

For the first time, Moses felt God's disapproval of him. It would be the first of many times that Moses would argue with his God, and God would listen to him. Patiently, the voice spoke.

"Is there not Aaron, your brother, the Levite?" the voice said. "I know that he can speak well. . . . He shall speak for you to the people and he shall be a mouth for you."

Moses had not seen or heard of his brother Aaron since he was an infant. Even the name was unfamiliar. But he felt happy within himself. God had understood and was sending someone to help him. He would not be alone in his mission.

CHAPTER VIII

Two Brothers

They met in the wilderness. Aaron had heard the voice of God come to him as though in a dream. He had left his family and set out for the desert, to the place where he would meet the younger brother he did not know.

It began awkwardly. The two men looked at each other without a spark of recognition. They might have been strangers—they were strangers, for all they knew and understood about one another.

Stiffly, the brothers kissed. A bit embarrassed, they talked first about themselves and the years that had gone by. Moses spoke of his life as a shepherd and his happiness with Zipporah and Gershom and his younger son Eliezer. He had taken his family with him when he left Midian and had put them up at an inn when he went to meet Aaron.

Aaron told Moses about the life he and their parents had led during the years that Moses lived in Pharaoh's court. Aaron had been six years old when Moses had left the Hebrew settlement. He remembered little about the incident except the look of anguish on his mother's face when the princess' servants came to take his baby brother away.

Like others in the tribe of Levi, Aaron had grown up to be a priest among the Hebrews. The Egyptians treated the priests somewhat better than the rest of the people, for fear of offending the Hebrew God. So Aaron did not have to slave at making bricks and buildings the way other Hebrews did.

He had to watch helplessly, however, as his people suffered and died at the hands of the Egyptians. He and his elder sister Miriam spent much time among the people, going from tribe to tribe and hut to hut, talking to them, comforting them, and trying to give them faith in the God of Israel. Aaron told Moses that the people respected Miriam. Sometimes they called her the Prophetess because she spoke and sang with such feeling about the God of Abraham, Isaac, and Jacob.

Both Miriam and Aaron were married. Aaron's wife Elisheba, he said proudly, had borne him four sons, Nadab, Abihu, Eleazar, and Ithamar.

Moses liked what Aaron said and the way he spoke. He had a soft, cultured voice, far different from the harsh, unmusical sounds most of the Hebrews made. He was handsome, too, in a gentle sort of way.

Slowly, Moses brought the conversation around to the reason for their reunion. He had not as yet spoken to anyone about his remarkable experience with the burning bush. To his father-in-law, he merely said that the time had come for him to return to Egypt, to see how his kinsmen were. Always a sensible and sensitive man, Jethro had not questioned Moses, but had simply bade him to "go in peace."

Now Moses told Aaron about his vision and about all the things God had said to him. As he spoke, he watched Aaron's face carefully. He had to make sure that this man truly understood, that he had not come to mock Moses or laugh at his description of the meeting with God. But Aaron listened quietly. Once in a while he asked a question, and from time to time he nodded slightly as Moses explained to him the words that God had directed them to say to the people of Israel.

When Moses finished speaking, Aaron looked at him with glowing eyes. More than Moses, he had known the misery of his people. He had lived with it day after day. With all his heart he now dedicated himself to his brother and to his God.

Together the men planned their first step. Aaron knew

all the elders of the tribes of Israel. He would prepare the way for Moses by speaking to them individually and in small groups. Then Moses would come and perform the signs that God had shown him.

During the next few weeks, Aaron and Moses made their way through the land of Goshen, speaking to the leaders of the twelve tribes of Israel. They moved slowly so as not to arouse the suspicions of the Egyptian over-seers. Mostly they met with the people at night, when the overseers slept or held rowdy parties.

To each tribesman, Aaron told the same story. In his earnest manner and fine way of speaking, he told about the God who had appeared to Moses and about the life of freedom and plenty that God had promised the people of Israel. When he finished speaking, Moses spoke, hesitat-ingly, in the slurred way he had, but with such fire in his voice that the people listened and believed what he said.

As time went on, the brothers gained many followers. Some elder tribesmen were drawn to them out of religious feelings, awed by Moses' vision of God. Many others saw these two brothers as Israel's only hope—its ultimate hope —of escaping from Egyptian slavery.

With the people supporting them, Moses and Aaron prepared for the second part of their plan. This was the hardest part, when they must face the Pharaoh of Egypt and speak the words that their God had commanded them to say.

CHAPTER IX

IN PHARAOH'S COURT

Nothing had changed. As he and Aaron walked through the long corridor leading to Pharaoh's throne room, Moses felt as though he had never been away. The same rows of brightly striped pillars lined the hallway and the same gay tapestries hung on the painted plaster walls. The ceilings were as blue as ever, as blue as the sky over Egypt, and the floors of patterned tiles sparkled up at them as they moved along. Dotting the sides of the building were the small, narrow doorways that the Egyptians had designed to keep out the sun. Even now Moses could find his way quickly through one of the doorways to the enclosed courtyard where he had played as a child. He could almost smell the sweetness of the fruits and flowers that filled the courtyard and feel the coolness of the shallow pool where he had splashed with his friends.

Long ago Moses had left all this luxury and beauty behind him. He was a different man now, both inside and out. His hair was sprinkled with gray, his beard long and bushy, and his face lined with age and care. Still, the familiar sights tugged at him, bringing back memories of his happy childhood.

Together the brothers entered the court. Following the practice of the Egyptians, they bowed low to the ground and praised the king's wisdom and beauty in the traditional words that Moses had remembered and taught Aaron.

Pharaoh barely looked at them. If he recognized Moses he did not say so. But it was his custom to allow his subjects to bring their complaints to him from time to time. In that way he made the people feel that he cared for them, and helped keep peace within the land.

With a motion of his hand, Pharaoh gave Moses and Aaron his permission to speak. Taking a deep breath, Aaron stepped forward. His lips looked dry and stiff as he said words that Moses had drilled into him.

"Thus says the Lord, the God of Israel," he began. " 'Let my people go, that they may hold a feast to me in the wilderness.' " Moses had instructed him to ask for a little at first and work up slowly to the demand for complete freedom.

With a sinking feeling, Moses heard snickers among Pharaoh's courtiers as Aaron spoke. We must sound foolish, he thought, to be asking the ruler of Egypt to allow hundreds of thousands of slaves simply to walk out of the country for a few days while they worshiped a foreign God. But he could not turn back.

Moses heard the Pharaoh answer in a voice filled with mockery:

"Who is the Lord, that I should heed his voice and let Israel go? I do not know the Lord, and moreover I will not let Israel go."

Moses could feel Aaron's eyes on him. Glancing at his brother, Moses nodded for him to go on.

"The God of the Hebrews has met with us; let us go, we pray, a three days' journey into the wilderness, and sacrifice to the Lord our God."

A heavy silence filled the room. Raising his eyes, Moses saw the king sitting stiffly on his throne, his face flushed with anger. They had gone too far. The joke was over as far as Pharaoh was concerned. He did not want to hear any more about their Lord, "the God of the Hebrews," who had "met" with them. From his point of view they were the lowest of the low. How dare they pretend to have spoken to a god, one whom Pharaoh knew almost nothing about!

"Get to your burdens," he shouted. Before they could answer, his soldiers ushered them out of the throne room, past the great colonnaded hall, through the double gate outside the palace, and onto the street.

Defeated, they walked back toward Goshen, preparing for their next round.

Behind them, Pharaoh, too, was making plans. It was obvious, he told his advisors, that the slaves did not have enough to do. Otherwise they would not have had time to plot ways to leave the country and to talk foolishness with these two so-called prophets. The way to stop these men before they stirred up any more trouble was to increase the work of the Hebrews and make it clear to them that their new burdens grew out of the demands of Aaron and Moses.

Pharaoh put his thoughts into effect immediately. During the next few days, all Egyptian overseers received new orders. Until then, the slaves had been given the straw that they needed to use as a binder in making their bricks. Now the slaves would have to search the land and find the straw themselves. But they must continue to produce the same number and quality of bricks as before. Anyone who did not produce his quota would be publicly beaten, as a lesson to all the others.

The order took the people by surprise. Overworked and underfed, they could not bear up to this new form of torment. Their spirits broken, they appealed to the Pharaoh for an explanation. The answer they received was carefully designed to cause trouble.

"You are idle," the Pharaoh said. "You are idle; therefore you say, 'Let us go and sacrifice to the Lord.' Go now, and work; for no straw shall be given you, yet you shall deliver the same number of bricks."

It was a clever plot, and it led to just the results Pharaoh wanted.

Moses and Aaron are to blame, the people told one another. It is the fault of Moses and Aaron and the elders who made us follow them.

In angry groups they marched on the hut that Moses and Aaron had made into their headquarters. Cursing and shouting, they surrounded the brothers.

"The Lord look upon you and judge," the people shouted, "because you have made us offensive in the sight of Pharaoh and his servants, and have put a sword in their hand to kill us."

For Moses, each word was like the stab of a knife. He had been a simple shepherd, content in his solitude. He had not wanted this mission—he had pleaded to be spared from it. The Lord had sought him out and forced him to return to Egypt. For what? To make his people suffer even more?

Aaron and some of the elders managed to calm the people and gradually they drifted away from the hut, turning around once in a while to shake their fists at Moses or spit on the ground as a sign of their disgust. Long after they were gone, Moses could see their angry faces in his mind and hear the shrill cry of their voices. "The Lord look upon you and judge."

Pained and bitter, with tears streaming down his face, he raised his eyes to heaven and cried out, "O Lord, why has thou done evil to this people? Why didst thou ever send me? For since I came to Pharaoh to speak in thy name, he has done evil to this people, and thou has not delivered thy people at all."

Then he heard the voice again, the same voice he had heard near the burning bush. This time it sounded angry, and determined.

"Now you shall see what I will do to Pharaoh," the voice said, "for with a strong hand he will send them out, yea, with a strong hand he will drive them out of his land."

CHAPTER X

Let My People Go

"Prove yourselves by working a miracle."

Pharaoh was testing them, and Moses knew it. Somehow he and Aaron had managed to arrange this second meeting with the king. He suspected that Pharaoh had agreed to the meeting in order to humiliate the brothers more than ever in the eyes of his people and theirs. But Moses was not afraid. He and Aaron had prepared themselves carefully for this moment.

"Prove yourselves," the Pharaoh was saying again. In spite of himself, he enjoyed matching wits with these two brothers.

Smiling slightly, Moses turned to Aaron, who stepped forward and bowed low before the king. With a flourish, Aaron raised the rod he was carrying high above his head and threw it to the ground in the way Moses had taught him many months earlier. In a split second, the rod turned into a huge, angry snake.

Glancing at Pharaoh, Moses saw that the king was smiling, and Moses smiled more broadly. Then he saw

57

the king throw his head back on the pillow of his throne and laugh almost uncontrollably. Soon the whole court was laughing and pointing at Aaron's twisting, hissing snake.

With a single gesture, Pharaoh called a group of men to his side. Moses recognized some of them. They were the magicians and priests whom the king always kept close at hand. These men had trained themselves in every manner of magic and witchcraft. They were experts at fooling the eye, and often they amused the king with the wondrous tricks they could perform. Mostly, however, they used their magic to frighten the people and in that way gain power for themselves and the Pharaoh.

As each man approached, Pharaoh whispered something to him, and the magician took his place in a kind of semicircle around Aaron's snake. When all the magicians were in place, each in turn lifted his rod and threw it to the ground. As each rod hit the ground, a snake appeared, and as each snake appeared, the laughter grew louder and louder.

Then, suddenly, it stopped. Before the bewildered eyes of Pharaoh and his court, Aaron's snake darted out at the snake next to it, opened its mouth wide, and quickly swallowed that snake down. Hissing and writhing, as though with a terrible anger, it repeated the same quick movement again and again, until it had swallowed every snake in the room. Its meal finished, the snake fell asleep.

There was no need to say anything. The message was clear. Without a word, Moses and Aaron left the palace.

But the battle was just beginning. After his first shock, Pharaoh was only mildly impressed with Moses' snake trick, as he called it. Certainly, he was not impressed enough to take seriously Moses' demand that he free the people of Israel. It would take months of arguing and pleading, of threatening and bargaining, before Pharaoh would give in to Moses.

For Moses, those next few months were among the most difficult of his life. Time and again he found himself punishing the people of Egypt in the name of his Lord and watching them suffer because of the stubbornness of their king. For all his dedication to his God and his people, Moses had no heart for seeing others—even his enemies—suffer. Again and again, he tried to reason with Pharaoh, to save him and his people from the anger and might of the God of Israel.

"Let my people go," were the words with which Moses and Aaron presented their case to Pharaoh at each meeting. Let my people go that they may serve their God. Let my people go that they may worship together. Let my people go that they may live like men and not like animals. *Let my people go.*

For the Pharaoh of Egypt, those words, "Let my people go," became the most hated words he would ever hear. Each time he heard them they were accompanied by a threat. And each time he refused to accept them, the threat came true. He and his countrymen had lived through many natural disasters during the course of his reign. They had suffered from drought, from epidemics among themselves and their cattle, from rainstorms and sandstorms. But the series of disasters and plagues that now came upon them, one after the other, had no equal in the history of their country.

CHAPTER XI

THE PLAGUES

First came the blood.

As Pharaoh and his servants strolled one morning along the banks of the Nile, Moses and Aaron suddenly appeared before them. To the Egyptians, Moses looked and sounded like a madman. His eyes were blazing, his rod waving angrily in the air, and his voice heavy with feeling.

"Let my people go," Moses cried out. "Thus says the Lord, 'By this you shall know that I am the Lord: behold, I will strike the water that is in the Nile with the rod that is in my hand, and it shall be turned to blood, and the fish in the Nile shall die, and the Nile shall become foul, and the Egyptians will loathe to drink water from the Nile.'"

Even as Moses spoke, Aaron raised his rod and brought it down quickly, striking the water of the Nile. In seconds, while the Egyptians looked on shocked and speechless, the water turned a deep red. Minutes later, dead fish began to float on its surface and to be washed up along the shore.

For seven days and seven nights, the blood that Moses and Aaron had brought on the waters of Egypt was everywhere. And the odor of the blood and the dead fish rose from the waters to choke the people and sicken them as they thirsted for a drop of clear water to cool their parched mouths and throats.

On the eighth day, Moses appeared before Pharaoh. One glance told him that in spite of the suffering, the king had not changed his mind. Rumor had it that Pharaoh's magicians had convinced the king that they, too, could turn water into blood, and Pharaoh had hardened his heart.

Without waiting for permission to speak, Moses began: "Thus says the Lord," he said, " 'Let my people go that they may serve me. But if you refuse to let them go, behold, I will plague all your country with frogs; the Nile shall swarm with frogs which shall come up into your house, and into your bedchamber and on your bed, and into the houses of your servants and of your people."

And so the second plague began. Aaron raised his rod over the waters of the Nile. This time there was no blood and no water. Just frogs. Thousands of frogs, hundreds of thousands of frogs leaped and crawled and jumped out of all the waters of the land. There were great frogs and small frogs, thin frogs and fat frogs. There were green frogs and yellow frogs and red frogs and brown frogs. In everything and over everybody the frogs came, so that the people could not bathe or eat or walk or sit without finding themselves crawling with frogs.

In disgust, Pharaoh called Moses to his palace.

"Entreat the Lord to take away the frogs from me and from my people," he said, "and I will let the people go to sacrifice to the Lord."

Delighted with his quick victory, Moses spoke humbly, not wishing to humiliate Pharaoh any further.

"Be pleased to command me when I am to entreat, for you and for your servants and for your people," he said softly, "that the frogs be destroyed from you and your houses and be left only in the Nile."

"Tomorrow," answered Pharaoh, dismissing Moses with a wave of his hand.

Tomorrow, however, was the same as yesterday and the day before. As soon as Moses had carried out his part of the agreement and seen to it that all the frogs were destroyed, Pharaoh changed his mind and refused to allow the people of Israel to leave the land.

With his refusal, a new plague struck Egypt. While piles of dead frogs still lay stacked up throughout the land, a siege of gnats swooped down on the Egyptians. The gnats came suddenly, out of the air and the dust of the earth. So tiny they could barely be seen, the gnats dug their way into man and beast. They stung and bit and scratched so that their victims' eyes and skin became red and swollen. They sucked and plucked and buzzed at the people's hair and mouths and eyes and ears until men and women screamed in agony and nausea.

As the days of the gnats wore on, hordes of people began to crowd outside Pharaoh's palace, pleading with him for help. Even his haughty magicians turned to him to beg for relief.

"This is the finger of God," they admitted. They had no match for this kind of magic.

But the stubborn Pharaoh would not listen and would not give in.

Flies came next. If the gnats had tormented the people, the flies were ten times worse. A person could not breathe or swallow without taking in a mouthful of flies. The flies covered everything—houses and furnishings and dishes and clothes. They ate the crops and pestered the animals and spread disease from household to household.

By now, Pharaoh and the Egyptians had discovered an amazing thing. While they and all their land suffered from the horrible plagues, the land of Goshen where the Hebrew slaves lived seemed to thrive. Pharaoh learned

from his overseers that there were no flies in the land of
Goshen. No flies, no gnats, and no frogs had plagued
the land of the slaves. The God of Israel, the mighty God
who was making the Egyptians suffer so, was protecting
His own people. That, perhaps, was the most frightening
part of the plagues.

Still, Pharaoh would not give in. It was not just because of the slaves. They had become so hateful to him
that he sometimes thought he would be glad to be rid of
them—them and their leader Moses. Giving in to Moses
and his God, however, meant more than just letting the
slave people leave the land. It meant recognizing and
accepting this God of Israel, the God of the fathers as the
slaves called Him. It meant admitting that this God was
mightier than all the gods of Egypt—mightier than the
Pharaoh himself, the god of gods. Pharaoh could not
bring himself to do that.

So the plagues continued. And the new plagues were
so horrible that the people of Egypt longed for the "comfort" of the gnats or the flies or the blood—anything but
the terror of the illnesses that now plagued them. First,
their cattle died. One day all their animals—sheep, cows,
camels, asses—died in the fields where they were standing.
Then, before anyone could cart away the dead carcasses or

clear the air of the stench of the animal bodies, the people themselves were struck down with a miserable illness of their own.

Boils. The body of every man, woman, and child in Egypt was covered with boils. Red and runny, swollen and painful, the boils itched and burned at the same time so that the people could not sit or lay down or lean their bodies on anything without crying out in pain. Nobody, not even Pharaoh or his magicians and priests, were spared from the plague of boils. But in the land of Goshen, the Hebrews were healthy and wholesome, untouched by the agony of the sixth plague.

The seventh plague seemed worst of all. In the middle of summer, while the Egyptians still suffered from their terrible boils, the skies opened up and a storm unlike any they had ever seen crashed down on their land. The earth shook with thunder and the skies lighted up with flashes of fire and lightning. Soon, as though the heavens themselves had been ripped open, torrents of hail rained down on the land. The hail was like huge balls bouncing onto rooftops and into fields. Nobody could escape the hail, the lightning, and the fire that devastated the land, the vineyards, the wheat fields, the houses and temples. Only in Goshen, the skies were quiet and the land peaceful.

This time Pharaoh could not stand it. The screams of

the people, the wail of dying animals, the crashing of buildings and trees—they were too much for him. Angry, hating himself and his gods in his defeat, he sent for Moses and Aaron.

"I have sinned this time; the Lord is in the right, and I and my people are in the wrong," he said quickly, not looking at the two Hebrews. "Entreat the Lord; for there has been enough of this thunder and hail; I will let you go, and you shall stay no longer."

"As soon as I have gone out of the city, I will stretch out my hands to the Lord," Moses said. "The thunder will cease and there will be no more hail, that you may know that the earth is the Lord's."

Then, sadly: "But as for you and your servants, I know that you do not yet fear the Lord God." Moses had little faith in Pharaoh's word. Still, there was the hope that the king was telling the truth, and that his people would be spared more suffering.

In a few hours that hope was shattered. As soon as the hail and thunder ended, Pharaoh changed his mind and went back on his word as Moses knew in his heart that he would.

Once again, as they had seven times before, Moses and Aaron appeared before Pharaoh, and Moses spoke in God's name.

"Let my people go, that they may serve me. For if you refuse to let my people go, behold, tomorrow I will bring locusts into your country, and they shall cover the face of the land, so that no one can see the land."

Once again Pharaoh refused.

Moments later the sky darkened and the roar of wings filled the air as great, black clouds of locusts, or grasshoppers, swooped down on the land of Egypt. Millions of locusts rested on the homes and fields of the Egyptians, eating everything in sight, everything that had not been destroyed by the hail. So many locusts filled the land that they covered the earth, making it look muddy and dark.

Again Pharaoh called Moses to him, promising to set the people free if the plague of locusts was lifted, and again Moses prayed to God to cure the land of its dreadful plague. A wind came and lifted away all the locusts. But once again, Pharaoh hardened his heart and refused to let the Israelites leave the land of Egypt.

The ninth plague came quietly. There was no thunder or lightning, no roar of wings, no crash of hail. Only darkness. The darkness descended on the land like a curtain, so thick it could almost be felt. For three days the darkness hung over Egypt, pitch-black darkness in which nobody could see an inch ahead of him. As the walls of darkness hemmed them in, the people cried out for help.

But there was nobody to hear them. Their great god Amon-Re, god of the sun and of light had been defeated. He and his priests had deserted them before the might of the God of Israel, and the people were left to stumble blindly on their own.

At the end of the third day, Pharaoh summoned Moses to him.

"Go, serve the Lord," he shouted at Moses. "Your children also may go with you; only let your flocks and your herds remain behind." He wanted some assurance that his slaves would be back, that they would stay away only three days, as Moses had said.

Moses answered quietly and firmly.

"Our cattle also must go with us; not a hoof shall be left behind, for we must take of them to serve the Lord our God, and we do not know with what we must serve the Lord until we arrive there."

Now the horror and hatred of all he had lived through gripped Pharaoh. His face twisted in rage, his voice rising higher and higher, he screamed at Moses, "Get away from me; take heed to yourself; never see my face again; for in the day you see my face you shall die."

"As you say!" Moses answered, turning his back on Pharaoh. "I will not see your face again."

CHAPTER XII

DEATH IN THE NIGHT

What Pharaoh wanted more than anything in the world now was to destroy Moses. Sometimes he awoke in the middle of the night, grinding his teeth and crying out his hatred of the Hebrew. Sometimes he sat in his throne room picturing in his mind torture and death for Moses. He would have the slave leader stoned to death, he told himself. First, however, he would make him suffer. He would make Moses bleed and beg for mercy the way Pharaoh had begged the God of Israel for mercy after the worst of the plagues.

It made Pharaoh happy to imagine Moses miserable and crawling for mercy. He laughed to himself whenever he thought about it. But the laughter was hollow. For all his daydreams, he knew that his hopes would not come true. He would not kill Moses or even harm him in any way. He dared not. He feared the Hebrew more than he had feared any man.

Moses was different from any man the Pharaoh had ever met. Even his snake trick had been different from

the tricks of the court magicians. As for the plagues, nobody, not even the high priest of Egypt, had been able
to imitate the series of plagues that Moses had brought
down on Egypt just by raising his rod or lifting his arms
to heaven.

Moses always spoke about his God. But Pharaoh wondered whether Moses himself was a god, come to earth
in the form of a man. If he was a god, how could Pharaoh
kill him or even hurt him? If he was not, then surely he
spoke truly and some mighty and invisible power—greater
than all the gods of Egypt—watched over him and protected him.

Every day Pharaoh's hatred of Moses increased, and
so did his fear. He searched endlessly for a way to end the
threats and plagues, a way to end the nightmare of the
bearded Hebrew with his magic rod and his priestlike
brother whose words came out smooth and soft, like
golden honey. When the days became worse instead of
better, Pharaoh's hatred and fear grew almost out of
control.

The last few days had been the worst of all. Moses
had left him in anger, and in the darkness that covered
Egypt, Pharaoh had waited. Day after day he had
waited, in darkness and gloom, to see what would happen
next.

While Pharaoh waited, his enemy Moses readied himself and his people for their final victory.

"Yet one plague more I will bring upon Pharaoh and upon Egypt," God said to Moses. "Afterwards he will let you go hence; when he lets you go, he will drive you away completely."

Moses had been alone in his hut when the voice of God came to him to describe that one last plague.

"About midnight," God told Moses, "I will go forth in the midst of Egypt; and all the first-born in the land of Egypt shall die, from the first-born of Pharaoh who sits upon his throne, even to the first born of his maidservant who is behind the mill; and all the first-born of the cattle. And there shall be a great cry throughout all the land of Egypt, such as there has never been nor ever shall be again. But against any of the people of Israel, either man or beast, not a dog shall growl."

The words were simple, almost matter-of-fact. But the act God described was so frightening that Moses could barely imagine it.

After a while, the voice had come to him again, and this time it told him in great detail how the people of Israel were to get ready for the day of their liberation.

On the tenth day of the Hebrew month of Nisan, each head of a household was to choose a young male lamb from his flock. He was to keep the lamb until the fourteenth day of the month and on that day he was to slaughter it. Each man and his family were to roast their lamb and eat it. Before roasting their lambs, however, the people were to dip a bunch of hyssop leaves into the blood of the animal, and with the leaves, draw a mark on their doorposts.

Every Hebrew doorpost must have a mark of blood, God told Moses. That mark would be a sign to God, as He went through the land at night, destroying the first-born of Egypt. "When I see the blood," the Lord said, "I will pass over you, and no plague shall fall upon you to destroy you, when I smite the land of Egypt."

For days after he heard the voice of God, Moses went through the region of Goshen, meeting with the elders of the tribes of Israel. Word for word, he repeated God's commands as he spoke to each group of elders.

To each group, too, he added an explanation of his own. The night of the tenth plague, Moses told the elders, would also be the beginning of freedom for them. On that night, they, who had been slaves and the sons of slaves, would become free men. And on that night, for the first time, the twelve tribes of Israel would become a single nation. Many things would happen to them over the years, after they left Egypt and made their way to the land that God had promised them. Always, however, they must remember this special night when God's angel of death would pass over their houses and save them from slaughter, and they must set this night aside and observe it as a holy festival.

Amazed and thrilled by all that Moses told them, the elders returned to their tribes to prepare the people for the days ahead. This time nobody doubted Moses' words. Nobody cursed him or laughed at him. The Hebrews had seen the grasshoppers and the boils, the flies and the gnats that had plagued the Egyptians. They had seen the curtain of darkness that had shut off the land of Egypt while they basked in sunshine. They did not completely understand about Moses and the invisible God who spoke to him. But they knew that a great power was at work to save them.

With a mixture of joy and dread, Moses and the people of Israel waited for the night of the tenth plague.

When it came, they were seized with terror.

Earlier in the evening the people had slaughtered their lambs and marked their doorposts with blood, just the way Moses had instructed them. Then they closed their doors tightly, and huddled together in their huts counting the minutes until midnight.

That moment was almost too much for them to bear. It was as though the earth itself cried out in agony as the people of Egypt discovered their dead. Long low moans became cries and then shrieks and then screams of horror. Crowded in their dismal mud huts, the slave people hid their faces and held their hands to their ears so as not to hear the misery of their masters.

In Egypt, the dead were everywhere. Pharaoh's eldest son was dead. So was the first-born of his cook, of his scribe, and of his court jester. Dead dogs and dead cats and dead rats littered the streets, and in the fields first-born lambs and colts and calves lay down dead. At the stroke of midnight, death invaded every household in the land of Egypt, and the sound and smell of death filled the air.

Through it all, the people of Israel stayed behind their blood-marked doors in the land of Goshen. Moses had told them to pack their belongings and prepare food for the journey out of Egypt. But they could not move. Their legs were stiff, and their hands were numbed by the terror of what had happened.

Suddenly, toward morning, the distant sounds of moaning and cries grew closer. From behind their closed doors, the Hebrews heard voices, thousands of crying, begging voices coming closer and closer. Opening their doors slightly, they could see the Egyptians—masses of Egyptian men and women crying and pleading, and running toward their huts.

"We are all dead men," the Egyptians were saying. "We are all dead men." The Hebrews must leave their land at once or they would all die.

As they spoke, the Egyptians shoved gold, silver, and clothing at the Hebrew slaves. They wanted nothing, only to be rid of these people who had brought the terrible plagues on them. They were willing to give up all they owned—their cattle, foods, treasures, anything—to free themselves forever of the slaves.

In the midst of the turmoil, Moses received word that Pharaoh wished to see him.

The man Moses saw as he entered the palace was not the same man he had left only a few weeks before. Pharaoh looked old—old and gray and beaten. His eyes were rimmed with red, and his shoulders bent hopelessly as he leaned over the body of his dead son.

His voice trembling, he sobbed, "Rise up, go forth from among my people, both you and the people of Israel; and go, serve the Lord, as you have said. Take your flocks and your herds, as you have said, and be gone."

Moses bowed slightly, then left the palace. By the time he reached Goshen, the Hebrew people had assembled, so sure were they of what Pharaoh would say to Moses. They were a motley group. The women carried children on their backs and the men had made packs out of the clothing and the goods that the Egyptians had thrown at them. They were talking, shouting, and laughing all at once as they streamed out of their huts to take their places in long lines behind Moses and Aaron and the elder tribesmen.

Slowly, in disorderly columns, the Hebrews began to move away from Goshen, out of the land of Egypt. As they moved along, the people began to sing. Someone took out a tambourine, and the people sang and danced as they made their way out of Egypt with their cattle, their children, and their newfound possessions.

Up ahead, at the front of the columns of slaves, marched Moses and Aaron. With them they carried a coffin containing the bones of Joseph. It was more than four hundred years earlier that Joseph had entered Egypt as a slave and had risen to become another Pharaoh's prime minister. Before he had died, Joseph had told his people that someday they would return to their homeland, and that when that day came they should take his remains with them. So now, Joseph, too, finally was leaving with his people on their march to freedom.

CHAPTER XIII

Across the Sea

The first flush of excitement died quickly. It was not easy to walk for hours under the burning sun, carrying heavy bundles and leading long lines of cattle. As the Israelites grew hot, tired, and thirsty, their laughter and singing came to a stop. They began to grumble among themselves, and to cast dark looks at their leader Moses.

That man Moses has no consideration, they told one another. Perhaps the God he always spoke about gave him enough strength to walk this way, barely stopping to rest or eat. But they were tired, and their bodies were worn from years of hard labor. Why could he not understand that?

And why, when he did call a halt, must he lecture to them? From the moment they had left Egypt, Moses had begun to lecture to them. Always it was the same. Over and over he told them about their God and about the miracle of the slaying of the first-born. And again and again he described to them the festival of the Passover that they must

78

celebrate in their new land in honor of their escape from Egypt.

Everything about their departure from Egypt was sacred, according to Moses, even the tasteless flat breads they had baked just after leaving the country. In their hurried preparations, they had quickly kneaded their dough without taking time to add the leavening, or yeast, that makes the dough rise. Once out of Egypt, they had baked their breads in the hot sun and eaten them as they marched along. The unleavened breads, which the people called *matzoth*, tasted stiff and dry, and made them thirstier than ever. And then Moses, to their surprise, had announced that these very breads would be considered sacred from now on. Every year, as they celebrated their Passover festival, they must bake unleavened breads just like these, as a remembrance of their journey out of Egypt.

Oh, he was a strange one, that Moses. Yes, he was clever and strong-willed, and filled with miracles. But he was hard and strange, with all his talk about their God and His festivals as they dragged along in the hot sun. Perhaps—just perhaps—they whispered to one another, things might be easier for them if Moses were not so hard and so devoted to God; if Moses were more like them.

Moses knew what the people said about him. He

realized how tired they were and how suspicious and frightened. But he had a mission to carry out, and to his mind that came ahead of anything, even ahead of his sympathy for the people. His goal was clear. He must teach them God's ways no matter how much they complained about that learning.

Moses was glad of one thing. The people knew little about the land around them. Few of them had ever traveled beyond Goshen, except perhaps to work on some Egyptian palace or temple, carefully guarded by overseers.

They did not know the route that Moses was following now. If they had known it, they certainly would have complained more than ever. Only he and Aaron and a few trusted young men he had chosen to help him knew that Moses was leading his people on the longest route possible out of Egypt toward the land of Canaan.

Moses had chosen that route carefully. The short route, which stretched along the coast of the Mediterranean Sea, would take the Israelites through the heavily armed territory of the Philistines. Moses had become familiar with those powerful, warring people during his days as a prince of Egypt, and he was certain that, given the opportunity, they would attack the Israelites. His people were not yet ready to fight. One attack and they might turn around and run back to Egypt.

The long route that Moses had decided on led through the desert, from one stretch of wilderness to another. It would take the people clear across the Sinai peninsula, past the Gulf of Aqaba and on up into the land of Canaan. It would take them, too, past that mountain—that special mountain in Sinai where Moses first heard the voice of God. Perhaps, without even recognizing it, that was Moses' main reason for choosing the roundabout route.

During the first part of their journey, Moses had led the people southward, from Goshen to Succoth, about thirty miles away. They had rested at Succoth and then moved on a distance until they came to the west bank of the Sea of Reeds, the northernmost tip of the Red Sea, near today's Suez Canal.

They arrived near the Sea of Reeds late in the day, and the people set up camp for the evening.

While the people rested, Moses decided, he would continue working out his plans for the march to the land of Canaan. First, however, he must choose the best time and spot to cross the Sea of Reeds. It must be a time when the tides would be low and the people would be able to wade across the shallowest part of the sea with little trouble.

As he sat in his makeshift tent drawing up his plans, Moses became aware of distant noises that seemed to come from the edges of the Israelite camp. For a while he paid little attention, deciding that the noise was just the sound of the people calling to one another. He would have liked to join them, speak to them, and comfort them the way he often had when they were slaves in Egypt. But he had too much to do, arranging their great march through the desert.

After a time, Moses realized that the noise had grown louder. It was so loud that it sounded like a great rumble, and in the midst of the rumble he kept hearing his own name.

Stepping from his tent to find out what the commotion could be about, Moses saw Israelite men and women running, shouting, and pointing excitedly to what looked like large black clouds in the distance. Other people were gathered in groups, staring fearfully in the direction of the clouds.

As Moses and the people watched, the clouds drew nearer, and as they approached Moses knew that what he had secretly dreaded had come to pass.

The Egyptians were after them! The dark clouds were clouds of dust and sand raised by Pharaoh's horses and chariots. Hundreds of chariots with hundreds of horsemen were racing through the desert raising the great dust clouds that seemed to blot out the evening sun.

In an instant, panic swept the tribes of Israel, and the anger and fear that had been building up since they left Egypt burst out at Moses.

"Is it because there are no graves in Egypt that you have taken us away to die in the wilderness?" they shouted at Moses as he watched the approaching clouds. "What have you done to us in bringing us out of Egypt? Is not this what we said to you in Egypt, 'Let us alone and let us serve the Egyptians'? For it would have been better for us to serve the Egyptians than to die in the wilderness."

All at once they were surrounding him, shouting, crying, and shaking their fists. Some called out to the God of Israel for help, while others knelt and prayed to the Egyptian gods they had learned to worship during their years of slavery.

Caught in the middle of the excited, screaming mob, Moses remained calm.

"Fear not, stand firm," he said in his thick voice, "and see the salvation of the Lord, which he will work for you today; for the Egyptians whom you see today, you shall never see again. The Lord will fight for you, and you have only to be still."

They were brave words and Moses truly believed them. But how? he wondered. How will the Lord show His might this time? The people were trapped at the edge of the sea. How could they escape the Egyptians?

Without moving his lips, Moses called in his heart to his Lord. Deep within himself he heard the voice—the voice of God that came only to him and to no one else.

"Lift up your rod," the voice said, "and stretch out your hand over the sea."

Breaking away from the angry mob, Moses moved toward the edge of the sea. Slowly he raised his hands high above the water. As he did so, a mighty east wind blew up over the sea, bringing huge foaming waves into the once-calm, marshy waters.

Minutes passed, and the wind howled over the sea, waves crashed into one another, and all around the skies turned dark as night. Gripped with terror, the people clutched one another, afraid to cry out for help.

As they stood there frozen in their places, the waves rose higher and higher, and the wind hissed and howled around them. Then, before their amazed eyes, the waters began to part. Farther and farther the waters drew apart, until they stood like towering walls on either side of the sea. And there, between the walls of water, lay solid land.

Head held high, Moses walked toward the land, motioning the people to come after him. Hesitatingly, Aaron followed Moses. Next came Joshua, one of the young men whom Moses had appointed as his assistant. After him followed the priests of the tribe of Levi and after them the people of the tribes of Reuben and Simon, Judah and Benjamin. Soon, all the people of Israel came rushing toward the land, pushing their flocks before them and holding tightly to their bundles and their children.

Faster and faster the people ran across the path of land, while the towers of water rose high on either side of them. Behind them, the Egyptian chariots drew closer and the Israelites could hear the steady beat of horses' hooves on the desert sands.

Just as the last Israelite reached the shore on the other side of the sea, the Egyptian cavalry entered the land path that the winds of God had blown open.

Once across the sea, the Israelites kept running and running as fast as their legs would carry them. But Moses stopped and stood at the shore, quietly watching the approach of the Egyptian chariots and horsemen.

The waters were still divided as Moses watched, and the wind still whistled and whined. But the land itself was no longer the sturdy, hard-packed land that the Israelites had crossed. The earth between the waters had turned into thick, sticky mud. Moses could hear the shouts and curses

85

of the Egyptians as their chariots sank into the thick mud and their horses slipped and tripped whenever they tried to move.

Then Moses heard the voice of God once more:

"Stretch out your hand over the sea, that the water may come back upon the Egyptians, upon their chariots, and upon their horsemen."

As though he had been waiting for the command, Moses raised his hand quickly. In a second, the great walls of water that had stood apart for the Hebrews crashed down on the Egyptians, drowning Pharaoh's entire army of horses, riders, and chariots.

Gradually the winds stopped, the waters grew calm, and the moon rose on a star-filled night. Across the Sea of Reeds, the Israelites gazed at the calm waters in disbelief. It was as though nothing had happened. The waters sparkled in the moonlight, and gentle waves lapped the shores. Everything was the way it had always been, except for one thing: beneath those gentle waters lay Pharaoh's finest cavalry regiment, destroyed by still another miracle of the God of Israel.

For many minutes the people stared at the waters. Soon one and then another began to smile and then all began to shout and to cry out their pride in Moses and their

God. Oh, that man Moses was a great and mighty man, they told one another. Never again would they doubt him. Let him lecture to them, scold them, and march them as long as he wanted to. He was a true miracle man, and they would follow him always.

Dancing and singing, they surrounded Moses, this time cheering him loudly in their gruff voices.

Shyly at first, Moses let himself be drawn into the happy shouting mass. His heart, too, overflowed with happiness and love of his God. And he, too, began to sing.

"I will sing to the Lord, for he has triumphed gloriously," he called out in his unmelodious voice. "The horse and his rider he has thrown into the sea."

The people laughed and clapped their hands and sang:

> *The Lord is my strength and my song,*
> *and He has become my salvation;*
> *This is my God, and I will praise Him,*
> *my father's God, and I will exalt Him.*
> *The Lord is a man of war;*
> *the Lord is His name.*

On and on the song went, and long into the night the people sang in celebration of their great victory. Moses' sister Miriam took out a tambourine and sang and played while the women of Israel danced around her. Over and over men and women shouted the refrain of the song, while the stars sparkled in the sky and the earth seemed to join in the sounds of their happiness:

Sing to the Lord, for He has triumphed gloriously,
The horse and his rider He has thrown into the sea.

CHAPTER XIV

"What Shall I Do With This People?"

The weeks passed slowly after the miraculous crossing of the Sea of Reeds. The farther the Children of Israel went from the spot, the more distant the whole incident became in their minds. Sometimes they even doubted that a miracle had taken place. Perhaps it was only the wind and the tides that had helped them, they mumbled among themselves. Perhaps Pharaoh had sent his weakest men after them, and that was why Israel had won its victory. Perhaps their God was not as powerful as Moses said. For if He was, why did He let them suffer in the desert, growing thirstier and hungrier as the days wore on?

Two months had gone by since they had left Egypt. Day by day their supplies had dwindled, and their fears had risen. A hundred times a day they came to Moses with their questions. A thousand times a week they brought him their complaints and their doubts.

"What shall we drink?" they would shout at him as soon as he ordered them to move on, away from an oasis where they had camped for a while.

89

"Would that we had died by the hand of the Lord in the land of Egypt," they would cry, when he walked among them after a long, tiring day. "You have brought us out into this wilderness to kill this whole assembly with hunger," they would accuse him again and again with hatred in their eyes.

The pattern was not new to Moses. It had been this way from the beginning. When things went well, the people honored him as though he, rather than the Lord, had brought them their blessings. The minute trouble appeared, however, they turned against him and blamed him for every possible misfortune.

And always when they were unhappy, they spoke about Egypt, as though that cursed land had been their home, as though they had lived happy, carefree lives there.

"We remember the fish we ate in Egypt for nothing," they would tell him, forgetting that the fish they had been given in Egypt was spoiled leftovers which their masters would not use. "We remember the cucumbers, the melons, the leeks, the onions, and the garlic."

And did they remember the beatings? Moses would think to himself. Did they remember how their newborn sons were torn from them and murdered, how their daughters were taken as handmaidens by the Egyptian overseers?

The changes in the mood of the people tortured Moses. Sometimes he grieved in his heart for them, praying to God that he alone might suffer for all of them. Other times he grew impatient with their complaints and their lack of faith.

How many times must the Lord prove Himself? he would say to Aaron and to young Joshua. By how many miracles must He show them His ways?

The miracles had come one after the other as their journey had unfolded.

Just three days after crossing the Sea of Reeds they had come to a lake whose waters were so bitter that neither the people nor the animals could drink it. Almost immediately the people had turned against Moses, blaming him for bringing them to this region of bitter waters. Guided by God's voice, Moses had pulled up a scraggly tree that stood near the lake and had thrown it into the waters. Immediately, the waters had turned sweet and cool, quickly quenching the thirst and the anger of the people.

Not long afterward a cry had gone up throughout the Israelite camp that the people were running out of food. Soon they would have nothing at all to eat. That evening, as though out of nowhere, a school of quail had flown up near the settlement. In no time at all, the people had captured hundreds of the birds and held boisterous feasts on tasty, roasted quail.

For a while the complaints had stopped and Moses had become a popular hero again. But not for long. As soon as the quail had given out, the mumbling and grumbling had started once more. Then had come another miracle— the one Moses never ceased to wonder at.

It had come in the morning, at dawn, while the air was still crisp with the night's coolness and dew lay gleaming over the earth. As the dew began to evaporate, the ground beneath it looked white, as though covered with frost. When the people looked closely, however, they found not frost but a kind of white seed covering the entire wilderness. The seed was small and round, like the seed of the coriander plant, and Moses and the people were able to scoop up seeds by the handful.

The people called the seeds *manna*. In almost no time, they learned to grind, bake, and boil the manna into many kinds of foods. The best part was that to each person the manna tasted like the food he most felt like eating at the moment. One person said it tasted like sweet honey wafers he had once eaten in Egypt. Another thought it tasted like fish fried in oil.

Every day since that morning, the people had found the manna covering the ground, waiting to be gathered and turned into nourishing food. The seeds seemed to drop from shrubs that grew in the wilderness. The miracle of it was, however, that the shrubs were few and far between, yet the seeds covered the entire ground day after day.

Things had gone well after the discovery of the manna. Moses and the Israelites had moved from the oasis of Elim to a place in the wilderness known as Sin, on southward toward Rephidim, a fertile region in the Sinai peninsula.

At first they had found fresh springs and had been content to feed on the manna and drink the water they discovered. But as they pushed deeper and deeper into the desert, the springs became scarce and the land drier than they had seen it anywhere before.

Now, again, the cries of the people began to fill Moses' ears.

"Give us water to drink," a mother pleaded with him, holding out a thin, sickly child with eyes as big as saucers.

"Give us water," sighed an old man whose face looked as shriveled and dry as the land around him.

Soon—as Moses knew would happen—the blaming, the name-calling, the regrets started. The people came to him in groups, as they always did when things went badly. They stood around him weeping, shouting, and pleading.

"Why did you bring us up out of Egypt," cried one

woman, repeating those words Moses had come to hate more than any others, "to kill us and our children and our cattle with thirst?"

"Why did you bring us up out of Egypt?" chanted others, and Moses could feel his patience ebbing.

"Is the Lord among us, or not?" shouted a young man, in a tone filled with mockery.

Moses could take no more. He called out to the Lord, "What shall I do with this people?"

The sound of his voice—usually gentle and kind—shocked the people. In an instant all complaints and cries stopped, and they stared at him with fear in their eyes. His face was turned toward heaven and his body trembled as though gripped by some unknown power.

Within moments, he faced them again. He was calm now, and his eyes searched the group until they rested on some of the elder tribesmen. Motioning to the elders to follow him, he walked a short distance toward a rock that jutted from the side of a mountain. Without a word, he raised his arm and brought his shepherd's rod down sharply on the rock.

As the Israelites watched in wonder, water began to trickle from the rock. Then it flowed. Then it gushed out in torrents. After a stunned silence, men, women, and children rushed over to the gushing stream, jostling one another for a good spot in which to enjoy the clear, clean water. For hours they stayed there, crowded around the rock, laughing, splashing, and taking turns at drinking and washing themselves.

Only later when they had had their fill of the water did somebody notice that Moses was not among them. Then somebody else remembered seeing him walk off alone shortly after the first trickle had started, his shoulders stooped and his head bent toward the ground.

CHAPTER XV

Israel's First Battle

One morning Moses awoke earlier than usual. He had had a restless night and his mind was troubled. They had camped at Rephidim for some days now, and it was time to move on. He must organize the people and convince them to continue their journey into the wilderness, no matter how difficult it was.

The camp was quiet. Overhead, stars still glistened in the sky. Underfoot, the ground felt damp with its mixture of dew and manna. The stillness calmed Moses. He liked to wake up ahead of the people, to enjoy a few moments of peace all to himself. Still, he felt uneasy. He had a vague feeling that some grave danger faced the Israelites. Shaking his head as if to put the unpleasant thoughts out of it, he began to walk through the camp, looking over his "flock," as he sometimes called the Israelites.

Suddenly, out of the darkness, a figure rushed toward Moses. It was a man—an elderly Israelite—streaked with blood and panting as though with his last breath.

The Israelites have been attacked, the man screamed in a voice so shrill that Moses could barely make out his words.

Attacked! It was the one thing Moses had dreaded more than anything else, even more than the thirst and hunger that constantly plagued the people. He had purposely led his flock into the wilderness, far away from the main trade routes and towns of powerful nations. But he had failed to protect them.

The attackers were swarthy, fierce-looking shepherds, the man told Moses. Armed with swords and stones, they had swooped down on the outskirts of the settlement, where mostly old people and stragglers camped. Before word could spread, they had stolen the people's possessions and taken many of their animals. Behind them the attackers had left wounded, frightened, dying men and women. The man thought he had heard the attackers speak about something that sounded like "Amalek," but he did not know what that meant.

Moses did. The Amalekites were warlike Bedouins who roamed the desert in search of good watering grounds for their sheep and cattle. Moses had seen some of them during his flight to Midian years earlier, after he had killed the Egyptian guard. He had kept out of their way

97

then, fearing that they might beat and rob him. And now they had beaten his people as they plodded through the desert, weak, tired, and hungry.

Moses could feel his ears and cheeks grow hot as anger rose within him. Quickly, he led the man into his tent, so as not to frighten the people around him. After seeing that the man's wounds were treated, Moses left him and made his way to Joshua's tent.

Young Joshua, the son of Nun, had become Moses' most faithful friend. Sometimes Moses even felt closer to him than he did to his brother Aaron. Joshua was tall and handsome. He had thick black hair and dark intelligent eyes. He followed Moses around the way a younger brother follows an older brother. He also cared for and protected Moses. When the people grumbled and complained, Joshua always stood beside Moses, ready to spring forward in case anyone tried to harm his leader. When Moses called for volunteers to go ahead of the company and search for good resting-places or usable water holes, Joshua always volunteered first.

Now Moses would put Joshua to his first test as a leader of the people. Moses told him all that had happened with Amalek. Looking closely at Joshua, he said quietly, "Choose for us men, and go out, fight with Amalek."

Before he could finish speaking, Joshua was on his feet, ready to carry out his assignment.

All during that day and evening, Joshua rounded up the strongest and most courageous men among the Israelites. Word of the Amalek attack had spread and the whole settlement was abuzz with excitement.

Surprisingly, this time the people did not blame Moses. The need to fight the enemy who had attacked them so stealthily united them. Every able-bodied man volunteered to join the battle, while older men and women set to work preparing weapons for their instant army.

Everything became a weapon. Shepherds' staffs were turned into bows, and sticks found lying in the wilderness were whittled into arrows. The people gathered as many stones as they could and put them into goatskin sacks to be carried by their warriors. Without hesitation, the Israelites also turned over to Joshua the swords and shields that they had taken out of Egypt.

At dawn the next morning, the Israelite army set out to find the enemy. Earlier, Joshua had sent spies to fix the exact position of the Amalekite tribesmen.

At the head of the fighting men of Israel marched Joshua. Alongside him were Moses and Aaron and a man named Hur, Moses' nephew. Moses would not lead the actual fighting, but the people knew that he would lead the battle in his own way.

As they neared the Amalekite camp, Moses grasped Joshua's hand, blessed him, and wished him well. Then with Aaron and Hur beside him, he climbed to a nearby hill where he could clearly watch the course of the battle.

The Amalekites had expected the Israelites. They stood ready, banners flying, spears and swords poised, bows taut. As Joshua and his men approached, the Amalekites let out a piercing war cry, and surged forward toward Israel's army.

The battle raged mightily. The Israelites lashed back at their foes with an anger and energy that the Amalekites had never seen before. With all the makeshift weapons at their command, the men of Israel hurled themselves into the fight. And when their weapons gave out, they fought hand to hand, fiercely, bitterly, relentlessly.

From his hilltop position, Moses watched the battle and the first of his men fall under Amalek's sword, watched with pride as the brave Israelite warriors fought. Slowly, so that all on the battlefield below could see him, he raised his hands high above his head, and prayed out loud to his Lord. Stretched between his hands was the rod of miracles, the same rod he had used to split the waters of the sea, the same rod he had used to strike water from the rock.

From the battlefield below, the Israelites could see Moses, his white shepherd's robes flowing around his body, his arms stretched high toward the heavens. The sight of their leader standing there, praying to their God, gave them new strength, and they fought with even more courage than before.

As the battle blazed on, Moses became a kind of beacon for the fighting Israelites. Whenever they looked up and saw his arms and his rod raised, they fought bravely and victoriously, confident that Moses and the God of Israel were behind them. From time to time, however, they saw Moses lower his arms. Then they became frightened. It seemed to them that God had deserted Moses and the battle was lost. Their spirits gone, they would begin to retreat and fall before the might of the Amalekites.

Moses realized what was happening. With every ounce of strength he had, he struggled to keep his hands raised as the morning hours passed and the hot afternoon sun beat on his head. At times he felt sick from the effort and he grew dizzy, as though the sun and the hills were whirling around him.

Finally, Aaron thought of a scheme. Together he and

Hur carried a huge stone to the place where Moses stood. The stone was big enough so that Moses could sit on it and still be seen by the army below. Stationing themselves on either side of their leader, each man took one of Moses' arms, and held it up high.

For hours they stayed in that position, Aaron and Hur supporting Moses' arms while the white-bearded leader called out to the God of Israel for help in His people's first battle. Down below, the warriors drew strength again and again from the sight of Moses and fought with a courage and power that even he did not know they had.

By sunset there was no longer any doubt about the outcome of the battle. Israel had won a great victory. The Amalekites had either fallen or fled before the might of the Children of Israel. A shout of joy went up throughout the ragged, exhausted Israelite army. Even the wounded joined in the shouting and cheering, forgetting for the moment their pain. Led by Moses and Joshua, the victors marched back triumphantly to their encampment.

CHAPTER XVI

At the Foot of the Mountain

After the battle with Amalek, Moses noticed a change in the Israelites. Although they still complained about every shortcoming, their complaints had a new tone. Rarely did they call out to the gods of Egypt, as they had so often done during the early days of their journey. More often they spoke about the God of Israel, as though they, too, had finally come to know Him and worship Him as Moses did.

Moses was leading his people into the heart of Sinai now, to the very region where he had first received his mission. He had been thinking about that place for weeks as they inched their way across hot, dry lands. He had been thinking about those days—so long ago, it seemed— when he had tended Jethro's flocks and lived a simple, peaceful life with his wife and sons. He had been thinking about the wilderness and the lonely hours he had spent there with no one to talk to except his sheep and goats. Mostly he had been thinking about the mountain—

103

that mountain of God where he had seen the flaming bush and heard the voice that changed his world.

He was taking his people to that mountain. He did not know exactly why. He knew only that they must go. This time they must stand at the mountain together, and together shape their future there.

The southern part of the Sinai peninsula, which Moses and the people of Israel entered after leaving Rephidim, is shaped like a triangle. Near its tip stands a volcanic mountain, called today Jebel Musa (Mountain of Moses). This mountain, many scholars believe, was the Mount Sinai of Moses' day. Here Moses and the Children of Israel arrived on the first day of the Hebrew month of Sivan, the third month after their Exodus from Egypt.

Shortly after their arrival, Moses left his tent early one morning while everyone else was still asleep. He made his way to the foot of the mountain, and began to climb up its side. He left lighthearted and young, like a youth filled with energy and happiness.

He had gone only a few feet up the mountainside when he heard the voice of God calling out to him, as it had done near this spot so many years earlier. As he had done then, he slipped his sandals off his feet and hid his face in his arms.

"Go to the people," the voice of God said to Moses,

"and consecrate them today and tomorrow . . . and be ready by the third day; for on the third day the Lord will come down upon Mount Sinai in the sight of all the people."

That was his answer. That was why he had brought the people to Sinai, why he felt forced to bring them here. Here, for the first time, God would show Himself to the people of Israel.

Tension mounted in the Israelite camp during the next two days. Order followed order as Moses bustled about, preparing the people to meet their Lord. They must wash themselves twice a day, he commanded them. They must wash their clothes—all their clothes—and make sure they did not soil any clean garments. They must clean their sandals, their hair, their fingernails, and their ears, and see to it that their children's clothes and ears and finger-nails were spotless. Once they had been dirty, unkempt slaves. Now they were free men about to become a nation. They must purify themselves outside and in.

By the morning of the third day, the Israelites could barely hold back their excitement and nervousness.

When they awoke that morning, the sky was black. In the distance they heard a loud rumbling noise, like the sound of thunder, and saw flashes of light streak across the sky. Frightened, they huddled in their tents, wondering whether they had done something to anger Moses and his God. Then they heard Moses calling to them, telling them to leave their tents and gather outside the camp. Reluctantly, one by one, the people stepped out into the blackness, into the wilderness where Moses waited for them. When all the people had assembled, Moses signaled them to follow him, and together they marched toward the mountain.

The closer they came to the mountain, the louder the noise grew. Great peals of thunder crashed through the air and bolts of lightning slashed the sky like huge knives ripping apart the heavens. Out of the midst of the thunder and lightning came a new sound, the strangest sound of all. It was a trumpet blast, loud and shrill, calling to them again and again.

Gripped by fear, the people stared at the mountain. They had never seen such a spectacle before. A thick cloud of smoke surrounded the whole mountain, hiding its bushes and trees from view. And behind the smoke there were flames, great red tongues of flame shooting out from deep within the mountain and filling the sky above with an eerie red glow.

The thunder and lightning, the shrill trumpet blasts, the menacing flames terrified the people more than ever. Men hid their faces in their arms, women hugged their children close to them, pleading and screaming pitifully. Even Joshua and Aaron drew back in fear, afraid to move near the flaming mountain. Only Moses remained calm, as he walked at the head of the congregation, closer and closer to the mountain of God.

At the edge of the mountain, Moses called a halt to the procession. Here, he told the people, was where they were to stand, while he went ahead into the mountain itself, close to the flames, the dark smoke, the sound of the trumpet—and the Lord.

Still frightened, the people stood at the foot of the mountain, watching worriedly as Moses disappeared into the thick cloud of smoke. Around them the noise grew louder than ever, and the sound of the trumpet pierced the air as though echoing and reechoing from one end of the earth to the other.

Then suddenly, all sound stopped. All movement stopped. The wind—the hot wind that always blows in the wilderness—died down and stopped. A stillness filled the earth, a stillness so complete that not a leaf rustled, not a bird nor an insect nor an animal moved.

On the slope of the mountain, Moses could feel the stillness around him, covering him like a thick blanket. He, too, stood still, waiting, while he sensed his people trembling behind him and his God hovering above him.

Out of the stillness it came. From the midst of the darkness he heard the familiar voice once more. Louder than ever before he heard it, speaking words never before spoken.

I am the Lord your God, who brought you out of the land of Egypt, out of the house of bondage.

You shall have no other gods before me.

You shall not make yourself a graven image, or any likeness of anything that is in heaven above, or that is in the earth beneath, or that is in the water under the earth. . . .

You shall not take the name of the Lord your God in vain. . . .

They must hear, Moses thought to himself. This time the words of the Lord were not for his ears alone, but for all the nation to hear. Would they understand? Would they accept these strict and unfamiliar words?

The voice from the mountain continued, louder than before.

Remember the sabbath day, to keep it holy. Six days you shall labor and do all your work; but the seventh day is a sabbath to the Lord your God. . . .

Honor your father and your mother, that your days may be long in the land which the Lord your God gives you.

You shall not kill.

You shall not commit adultery.

You shall not steal.

You shall not bear false witness against your neighbor.

You shall not covet your neighbor's house; you shall not covet your neighbor's wife, or his manservant, or his maidservant, or his ox, or his ass, or anything that is your neighbor's.*

As suddenly as it had started, the voice stopped speaking. In an instant, the magic spell of stillness ended, and the world went about its business again. Slowly Moses turned and walked down the mountain, back to his people.

The Israelites were standing where he had left them. They looked the same, and yet they looked different. Moses could not tell how much they had heard and how much they had understood. No matter. He would carry the words of God directly to them.

As Moses approached, a loud cheer went up throughout the congregation. People ran over to embrace him. Some fell on their knees before him, others just stood still and cried uncontrollably. The noise and the stillness, the strange sights and the sounds had filled them with terror. But their leader was back and they were safe again.

When order was restored, Moses spoke to the people. They had never heard him speak so solemnly. He ex-

---

* For a listing of the Ten Commandments as given in the Protestant, Roman Catholic, and Jewish versions of the Bible, see the Appendix.

plained to them the meaning of what had taken place.

The Lord had proposed a contract—a covenant—with them this day, he explained. If they would accept the words of the Lord and the commandments He gave them, He would make them a great people, a holy nation. These laws, which the Lord had spoken from Mount Sinai, were the first part of the contract, the first Ten Commandments which they must obey.

In a loud voice, so that all could hear and understand, Moses repeated the commandments he had heard. As he spoke each one, he explained a little of what that commandment would mean to the people.

"You shall have no other gods before me," Moses repeated the words of God. That meant that the people could never again worship the gods of other nations—never. They could not bow down to the animals of Egypt, or sacrifice their children to the god Moloch, the cruel god worshiped by many desert people. They could not make images out of stone and brick, as other people did, and worship those images.

"You shall not kill." Did they know, Moses explained to the people, that killing meant more than just murdering another person? It meant that they must not injure or beat or in any way hurt one another.

"Honor your father and your mother. . . ." And your

teachers and the elders of your tribes, and all others who are older and more learned than you, Moses told the people. For with age comes wisdom, and wisdom is worthy of the honor and respect of all people.

On and on Moses went. One after the other, he repeated the commandments of God, and one after the other he explained them to his people. As he spoke, he walked through the congregation, stopping to address one person, to nod to another, to look for some sign of understanding on the face of another. He could not expect them to understand everything right away, but would they understand any of it? Could they rise above their lowly background of slavery and ignorance and believe in his words?

He had reached the last commandment, "You shall not covet your neighbor's house."

Amen, he heard a voice say.

Amen, chimed in another, and then another, and then another.

"All that the Lord has spoken we will do," called out a young man.

"And we will be obedient," added an older man.

Suddenly they were all shouting and speaking at once. They accepted the covenant with the Lord. They accepted the Ten Commandments. They had seen the glory and wonders of the Lord, and they would obey Him. Like a refrain, they repeated the words of agreement, and those words were the sweetest Moses had ever heard: "All that the Lord has spoken we will do, and we will be obedient."

With happiness filling his heart, Moses raised his head to heaven and thanked the Lord for this day. His eyes shining, he looked at the people around him, their faces reflecting his own joy. In his mind's eye, he saw not a band of shepherds gathered in the desert, but a huge assembly of peoples. He saw thousands and thousands of people of every nation and every time—young people and old people, kings and paupers, the dying and the unborn —joining in the contract with the Lord, and dedicating themselves with the same words his people had used:

"All that the Lord has spoken we will do, and we will be obedient."

CHAPTER XVII

AT THE TOP OF THE MOUNTAIN

"Tarry here for us, until we come to you again," Moses told the elders of Israel one day. "And behold, Aaron and Hur are with you; whoever has a cause, let him go to them."

Moses was leaving the Israelite camp for a while to go to the top of the mountain. He did not know how long he would be gone or just what he would do at the mountaintop. He knew only that he must go. Deep within himself he had heard the voice of God calling to him and he was obeying that voice.

With Joshua at his side, he walked briskly along the familiar path to the mountain of God. At the foot of the mountain, he bade farewell to Joshua, instructing the youth to wait for him there until his return. Never looking back, he began to climb upward. This time he would not stop part way up the side. He was headed for the summit.

Thick clouds covered the mountain as Moses pushed his way ever higher, ever closer to the top. His feet seemed to have wings on them, and his body felt light and free, as though he were floating on air. Higher and higher he climbed, into the heart of the clouds. Higher still he went, until he could see a flame at the top—like the flame that had burned in the bush and the one that had lit up the mountain on the day of the Ten Commandments.

At the edge of the flame Moses knelt, his head bowed low to the ground. In every part of his body he felt the presence of the Lord, and with all his heart he gave himself up to the majesty of the moment.

The day passed into evening and evening became morning, and then another day came and went. Then another and another. Forty days and forty nights in all, Moses stayed on the mountain, close to the flame and the thickness of the clouds. For him the time was like a second but also like a century. He sensed no hunger, no thirst, none of the everyday feelings that fill the lives of all men. Alone on the mountain, with nobody to disturb him, his mind seemed to open wide, to think and understand with a wisdom beyond anything he had ever known. Clearly he saw the lessons and laws he must teach his people as they journeyed to the land of Canaan.

"If a man steals an ox or a sheep, and kills it or sells it, he shall pay five oxen for an ox, and four sheep for a sheep."

"If you chance to come upon a bird's nest . . . you shall not take the mother with the young."

"A woman shall not wear anything that pertains to a man, nor shall a man put on a woman's garment."

Into every area of life Moses' mind and thoughts went. He seemed to sense every problem and every question the people would face when they finally lived together in their own land.

At the end of forty days, Moses was ready to leave the mountain. His face glowed with happiness and holiness. In his head he held the knowledge and teachings he would bring to his people. And in his hands he carried a special gift to them: the Ten Commandments carved in stone. The commandments were carved on tablets of stone, with each word chiseled deep into the stone so that it could not be rubbed out, not forgotten. Moses had worked on the stone tablets there at the mountaintop and while he worked it seemed to him that not his hands, but the finger of God shaped every word and every letter, making them perfect.

Like so many precious jewels, Moses carried the stone tablets of the law before him as he went down the mountain. This was his most sacred gift from the Lord to the people of Israel.

CHAPTER XVIII

SINNERS AT SINAI

"Make us gods!"

A group of the roughest, toughest Israelite shepherds stood before Aaron. Their voices were gruff and fierce, and they waved their shepherd's staffs threateningly as they spoke.

"Make us gods. . . . As for this Moses, the man who brought us up out of the land of Egypt, we do not know what has become of him."

They were angry. They had waited and waited for Moses to return from Mount Sinai. When the weeks passed and he did not return, they had become convinced that he had run away from them or died on his fiery mountain. What other explanation could there be for his long absence? He had promised to lead them to a wonderful land flowing with milk and honey and instead he had left them in the dangerous wilderness.

So they stood before Aaron, their staffs waving and their voices angry and urgent. They wanted new gods to worship, gods they could see and feel.

Soft-spoken Aaron, Aaron the peacemaker, the gentle priest, had to decide what to do. If he gave in to the people and made an idol for them, he would commit a grave sin against his brother and his God. But if he refused, they would kill him. Surely, they would kill him.

"Take off the rings of gold which are in the ears of your wives, your sons, and your daughters, and bring them to me," Aaron told the shepherds.

It was an attempt to avoid trouble. He would make a golden statue for them, like the statues of the Egyptians. To get it, though, they would have to sacrifice their most valuable possessions, the rings, bracelets, and ornaments they had taken from the Egyptians just before leaving that land. He could not imagine that they wanted an idol so badly that they would willingly give up the jewelry they dearly loved.

He did not know his people. Within hours, the men returned to him with basketfuls of jewelry. They had gone throughout the settlement collecting the peoples' gold ornaments. Those who refused to turn over their rings or necklaces were threatened and ridiculed. But most of the Israelites gladly gave up their possessions, so caught up were they by the promise of a new god.

Sadly Aaron melted all the gold he received. Slowly he molded the melted gold into the form of an animal. The people watched his every move. And when they saw the animal-god he had created, they let out a great cry of joy. It was a golden calf, similar to the golden bull Apis, a sacred god of Egypt. They had a golden calf that they could see, and touch, and worship, the way all the peoples of the world worshiped. No more of their invisible God and this Moses with all his laws and commandments.

"These are your gods, O Israel, who brought you up out of the land of Egypt!" a voice called out as the mobs stood around watching Aaron put the finishing touches on their golden god.

Suddenly the camp was in an uproar. Some of the men built a fire and others slaughtered a goat and offered it as a sacrifice to the golden calf. Girls stripped themselves bare to the waist and danced before the idol the way they remembered seeing girls in Egypt dance at religious ceremonies. Men and women sang at the tops of their lungs—songs about the Nile and the Egyptian gods, bawdy, unmusical songs they had sung as slaves in Egypt.

At the foot of the mountain, Moses heard the commotion. He had climbed down the mountainside and was standing with Joshua at the spot where he had left his assistant, when he heard the clamor.

"There is a noise of war in the camp," Joshua said to Moses.

"It is not the sound of shouting for victory, or the sound of the cry of defeat, but the sound of singing that I hear," said Moses.

His heart beat quickly. Something is wrong, his mind told him.

Together Moses and Joshua hurried to the camp. The scene they saw when they reached it would remain with Moses for the rest of his life. In the center stood the golden calf. Whirling around it were men, women, and children, dancing, jumping, and singing as loudly as they could. Some of the people carried fruits and wine as offerings to the idol. Others thumped on tambourines, setting the beat for the dancers who went faster and faster around the golden statue, as though in a trance. On the side stood Aaron, looking on in horror at what he had caused, and gathered around him were other members of the tribe of Levi, the tribe of the priests.

Shaking with rage, Moses stalked into the center of the camp, into the midst of the singers, the naked girls, and the worshiping people. With a cry of anguish that rose from deep inside him, he hurled the two stone tablets he had carried with him to the ground and watched as they shattered into a dozen pieces. Strengthened by his fury, he grabbed the golden calf and threw it into the fire. In silence, he watched the statue begin to melt. Around him, too, there was silence now as the people stood stunned and terrified at Moses' anger.

With his eyes Moses sought out his brother Aaron.

"What did this people do to you that you have brought a great sin upon them?" he shouted. He had left Aaron in charge of the camp. He must be held responsible for what had happened.

"Let not the anger of my lord burn hot," Aaron replied meekly, not daring to look his brother in the eye. "You know the people, that they are set on evil."

Yes, he knew the people. He also knew that they could be controlled. Why had Aaron been so weak? Moses could hardly listen as Aaron began a long-winded excuse.

". . . And I said to them, 'Let any who have gold take it off,'" Aaron explained, "so they gave it to me, and I threw it into the fire and there came out this calf."

". . . there came out this calf." The words infuriated Moses. Did the calf suddenly hop out of the flames? Why could not Aaron even admit that he had fashioned the calf, had given the people this false idol to worship?

In disgust, Moses walked to the edge of the crowd. Loudly he called out to the people:

"Who is on the Lord's side? Come to me."

Almost as a man, all the members of the tribe of Levi walked to Moses' side. They were the only tribesmen who had not taken part in the sinful celebration, who could truthfully say they were on the Lord's side.

"Thus says the Lord God of Israel," Moses said to them. " 'Put every man his sword on his side, and go to and fro from gate to gate throughout the camp, and slay every man his brother, and every man his companion, and every man his neighbor.' "

It was a horrible, cruel form of punishment. In later years people would look back and wonder how Moses, even in anger, could send his priests out to kill his own people. He did not want to, and yet he could not stop himself. It was the only way he could think of to cleanse the evildoers from the tribes of Israel.

During the rest of the day and the night, Moses stayed in his tent. Outside he could hear shouts and screams as groups of Levites sought out troublemakers who had roused the people. Later he was told that they had slaughtered three thousand men in all. He could not think of a worse day in his life, not even when he had murdered the Egyptian or had seen the tortured face of Pharaoh as his first-born son lay dead before him. In his anger he had destroyed the most cherished gift his people would ever have, the sacred tablets of the Ten Commandments. He had shouted at his brother and had sent his tribesmen out to kill. Worst of all, he had seen his people sin, and the memory of their trancelike faces as they danced around the golden calf tore at him as nothing else did.

Early the next morning he rose up and left his tent. His anger had left him. He felt nothing, only old and tired as he walked toward the mountain of God. At the foot of the mountain, Moses knelt and spoke.

"Alas," he said softly, "this people have sinned a great sin; they have made for themselves gods of gold. But now, if thou wilt forgive their sin . . ."

He could not go on. "If," he had said. And what if not? If God did not forgive, would He destroy this people He and Moses had cared for?

". . . And if not," he began again, "blot me, I pray thee, out of thy book which thou hast written." Destroy me, he thought. Erase my name from the Book of Life. But let Israel live.

From out of the mountain came the familiar voice, filling Moses' being.

"Whoever has sinned against me, him will I blot out of my book. But now go, lead the people to the place of which I have spoken to you; behold my angel shall go before you."

The words were like soothing oil to a man who has been

badly burned. They could mean only one thing. Somehow the people would be forgiven. Both he and they would live on.

CHAPTER XIX

Dos and Don'ts

Once more, Moses returned to Mount Sinai. With him on his long climb he carried two tablets of stone, shaped just like the ones he had broken in anger. The sacred words of the Ten Commandments would be chiseled on these tablets at the top of the mountain, where Moses felt himself free and alone with God.

Once again, Moses stayed on the mountain forty days and forty nights, unconcerned by the cares and needs of the ordinary world. When he returned this time, his face shone more brightly than ever. To his people it looked as though rays of light streamed from his head, surrounding him with so much brightness that they had to hide their eyes when they spoke to him.

For Moses, the second trip was even better than the first. He was calmer this time, and his mind was sharper than ever. Like a student sitting at the feet of his teacher, he sat on the mountain and felt himself surrounded by the spirit of the Lord. When he returned with the stone tablets, he walked with confidence, sure of himself and of the laws he had brought his people.

Life settled down after the excitement of the Ten Commandments and Moses' second journey to the heights of Sinai. The Israelites lingered in the region of the mountain, caring for their herds, rearing their families, and preparing themselves for their new land.

As he had done from the moment they left Egypt, Moses went among the people, teaching them the rules and commandments—the dos and don'ts—they had agreed to accept.

They learned slowly. All their lives they had lived in a land where only the rich and powerful counted for anything. Nobody paid much attention to how the common people treated one another or were treated by kings and noblemen.

Now everything the people did seemed to be important. Moses cared about what they ate, how they spoke to one another, even how often they bathed. More than that, he treated all men equally, as though each person in himself were important—the children as much as the old people, the lowliest member of a tribe as much as its most respected elder.

Even in his busiest hours, Moses always had time to care

about the weak. He instructed the people in how to behave toward the poor, the widow, the orphan, the servant, the blind—persons who in other countries would be neglected or sold into slavery.

"You shall not afflict any widow or orphan," he would command the Israelites in the name of the Lord. "If you do afflict them . . . my wrath will burn, and I will kill you with the sword, and your wives shall become widows and your children fatherless."

Or—

"When you reap the harvest of your land, you shall not reap your field to its very border . . . and you shall not strip your vineyard bare," he would tell them when they spoke about the land they would live in. "Neither shall you gather the fallen grapes of your vineyard; you shall leave them for the poor."

Or—

"You shall not oppress a hired servant who is poor and needy," he would instruct them. ". . . You shall give him his hire on the day he earns it, before the sun goes down, for he is poor and sets his heart upon it."

Or—

"You shall not curse the deaf or put a stumbling block before the blind," he would order, explaining to them

126

that deaf and blind also meant the simpleminded or innocent who were blind to the ways of the world.

Even foreigners and slaves received Moses' special
attention. During the months since they had left Egypt,
many wandering shepherds and Bedouins had joined the
Israelite tribes on their march to the Promised Land.
Moses was determined to have his people treat these
strangers well, both in the desert and in the Israelites' new
land.

"You shall not oppress a stranger," he told them again
and again. "You know the heart of a stranger, for you were
strangers in the land of Egypt."

As for slaves, what he had to say about them struck
the people as the most puzzling of all Moses' laws. They
found it easy to forget—they wanted to forget—their
sufferings in Egypt. They looked forward to becoming
like all the nations of the world, to having slaves serve
them the way they had served the Egyptians.

Moses would have it otherwise. He did not forbid them
to keep slaves. He could not, because slavery was a part
of the life of his times. But he went out of his way to
protect the slaves that the people might take.

"When a man strikes the eye of his slave, male or
female, and destroys it, he shall let the slave go free for the

eye's sake. If he knocks out the tooth of his slave, male or female, he shall let the slave go free for the tooth's sake."

And further, Moses commanded in the name of God, "You shall not give up to his master a slave who has escaped from his master to you; he shall dwell with you, in your midst . . . you shall not oppress him."

These were difficult laws to understand for a people whose children had been torn from them and murdered at the whim of their masters. Had the Egyptians, the Assyrians, or the Babylonians known of Moses and his laws about slaves, they, too, would have found these laws strange. In their lands, slaves were like property, to be handled the way a person wished. A master was as free to beat his slaves as he was to beat his horse or his ox. Yet Moses insisted that a slave must be set free if his master injured him, and instead of ordering punishment for runaway slaves, he commanded his people not to oppress them.

Not only that. Moses allowed slaves a day of rest, just as their masters had. The seventh day of the week, Moses taught the Israelites, was "a sabbath to the Lord." On that day, *all* living beings were to stop work and rest.

". . . You shall not do any work, you, or your son, or your daughter, or your manservant, or your maidservant," he told them. ". . . Your manservant and your maid-servant may rest as well as you."

And the seventh year was a special sabbath for slaves, Moses taught. After seven years of servitude, a slave was to be set free, no matter whether he was a man who had sold himself into slavery to pay off a debt, a slave captured in battle, or a person born into slavery. If the slave did not want his freedom—if he loved his master or was afraid to make his way alone in the world—he could choose to remain a slave, on one condition. His master was to pierce a large hole in his earlobe as a sign for all the world to see that he had heard the offer of freedom, and of his own will had given up this precious right and chosen slavery in-stead.

Strange laws, indeed. About five hundred years before Moses' time another great leader had given his people a set of written laws. His name was Hammurabi, and the laws he taught his people—the Babylonians—influenced all the nations that came after them. Moses must have heard of those laws while he was in the court of Egypt. Ham-murabi, too, taught his people not to steal, and not to murder or harm one another. And he, too, had special laws about the treatment of slaves. He even gave his people a law involving a slave's ear. Hammurabi's law stated that a slave was to have his ear cut off if he did not accept his position as a slave and obey his master. Moses' law stated that a slave's ear was to be marked if he did not accept his freedom and leave his master. A world of difference lay between Hammurabi's and Moses' laws, and the two ways of thinking they represented.

Behind all the rules and regulations that Moses taught the Israelites to observe in their dealing with one another and with other people was one simple commandment. If they understood and acted on that commandment, he explained to them, all the others would come easily. If they did not follow it, nothing else mattered. That commandment was "You shall love your neighbor as yourself."

Love also formed the basis of the people's behavior toward their God in Moses' system of law. "And you shall love the Lord your God with all your heart, and with all your soul, and with all your might," he taught them.

He said the words to the people often, as though repeating them would make the Israelites feel the same love that he felt for their God. Nevertheless, he knew that before they could love their God, they would have to accept Him as the one and only God of all the universe. And that was the hardest task of all.

There was not one nation in the world at the time in which Moses lived whose people believed in a single, all-powerful god. Like the Egyptians, the people of every nation worshiped many gods. The statues they built, the pictures they painted, and the ceremonies they performed in worshiping their gods differed from nation to nation. Almost always, however, the people imagined their gods to be much like human beings, or even like animals. They pictured the gods fighting among themselves, laughing, crying, loving, and hating just the way men and women do.

Once, an Egyptian king named Amenhotep IV tried to get his people to give up their worship of many gods and believe in one god. The god Amenhotep worshiped was the sun, which he called Aton. He changed his own name to Akhenaton, and told his people that he was the son of Aton. For many years, Akhenaton forbade the worship of many gods and ordered the Egyptians to worship only the sun-god. After he died, however, the people quickly returned to their old religion and their belief in many gods.

Moses surely knew about, and perhaps respected, Akhenaton and his belief in the one god of the sun. But Moses went much further in his beliefs. The God he taught his people to worship was an invisible God, unlike the sun whose rays could be seen and felt. The one true God, Moses said, was special and different, set apart from everything that people are familiar with in their lives. He does not look like a lowly animal, or even like the most beautiful person in the world. He is wise—wiser than the most learned man on earth. He is good—better than the most honest person alive. He is powerful—stronger than the strongest element in the universe. He is everywhere—above the heavens and below the earth.

Instead of animals and statues, Moses gave his people an idea. And because ideas are harder to accept than material things that can be seen and felt, it took the Israelites many many years to understand and truly believe in the idea of one, invisible, all-powerful, all-knowing God. Their hesitations and suspicions often angered Moses and made him impatient. He never doubted, however, that one day his idea of God would take hold of and guide his people.

CHAPTER XX

A MAGNIFICENT TENT

About six months after their arrival at Sinai, Moses gathered all the tribes of Israel for a meeting.

"Take from among you an offering to the Lord," he told them in a loud voice. His eyes sparkled and his face looked flushed with excitement.

"Whoever is of generous heart, let him bring the Lord's offering:

"gold, silver, and bronze;

"blue and purple and scarlet stuff and fine twined linen;

"goats' hair, tanned rams' skins, goatskins;

"acacia wood . . ."

The people listened in amazement to the words of Moses. Nobody had forgotten the terrible incident of the golden calf. If Moses did not remind them, the priests did, time after time. They remembered only too well how Aaron had collected their earrings and bracelets to melt into a crude golden idol. Here was Moses calling on them again for their jewelry, their gold, and their silver. Was he planning to make an image after all, a likeness of the God of Israel?

"Oil for the lamps, spices for the anointing oil and for the fragrant incense, onyx stones, and stones for setting," Moses went on, smiling at the people's puzzlement.

Yes, they were going to build something, but not a lowly statue or a forbidden idol. They were going to build a magnificent tent—a tabernacle—to hold their most precious possession, the tablets of the Ten Commandments.

Moses had received instructions from the Lord for building the tabernacle, he told the people. He had spent weeks planning the structure, down to the tiniest detail. The time had come to start building it.

While the people milled about, talking excitedly about the tabernacle, Moses appointed a young man named Bezalel, the son of Ur, to serve as chief designer and architect. The boy was a grandson of Moses' sister Miriam, a quiet, serious lad with large dark eyes and long, thin hands. To assist Bezalel, Moses chose a bouncy, talkative youth named Oholiab, the son of Ahisamach, from the tribe of Dan. Neither boy had received any artistic training, but both had such natural ability that people said they must be filled with the spirit of God.

During the next few days, the people of Israel brought their donations to the tents of Bezalel and Oholiab. There seemed to be no end to their offerings—gold and silver, bronze, precious and semiprecious stones, purple and blue dyes, perfumed oils, fine linen. Many of their gifts were things they had taken from the Egyptians when they left the land. Others were objects they had received in trade from nomads and caravan merchants they had met during their months in the desert.

By the end of a week, Bezalel's tent overflowed with so many precious goods that he had to appeal to Moses for help.

"The people bring much more than enough for doing the work which the Lord has commanded us to do," Bezalel said. Would Moses please put an end to the offerings so that he could get down to work?

By the end of the second week, the camp was organized. Bezalel put the men to work carving long poles out of acacia wood, building the framework for the tabernacle, and tanning rams' skins and goatskins for the tent covering. He assigned the women to weave curtains of goats' hair and to embroider linen with colorful designs. Bezalel allowed only the most skilled women to work with the valuable purple and blue dyes he had received. The dyes came from Phoenician traders, and were the most highly prized coloring in the world. The Israelites did not know the secret of making the dyes but they knew that in other lands these coloring matters were used only for kings and noblemen.

Bezalel reserved the hardest and most important work for himself, making the Ark of the Covenant that would hold the tablets of the law. He shaped the ark like a long chest and made it out of acacia wood covered inside and out with gold. It had a solid gold lid and two gold figures, called cherubim, with wings spread wide across the lid. Later, the lid with its cherubim became known as the mercy seat, and there, people believed, the spirit of God lived.

Together Bezalel and Oholiab designed another sacred object, a huge golden candlestick with seven branches. Bezalel drew the design for the candlestick. Then the two men built a metal mold into which they poured molten gold. When the gold hardened, they carefully removed the mold and put the finishing touches on the candlestick.

For six months, work on the tabernacle and its various parts went on. Moses had never seen the people so happy. Every tent hummed with activity, as men, women, and children dedicated themselves to their special projects. Bezalel, in his quiet way, seemed to have a gift for organizing the people, Moses noticed, so that each one had just the right assignment for his particular skills.

On the first day of the first month beginning the second

year after their exodus from Egypt, Moses and the people of Israel raised their holy tabernacle. It was the most beautiful structure they had ever seen. It stood in a large court, closed off by brass poles and richly embroidered curtains. In the court, outside the tabernacle, stood an altar on which they would offer sacrifices to the Lord. The altar was in the shape of a wooden box and overlaid with gold. Four golden horns jutted from its four corners. Near the altar a large copper washbasin held clear cool water which the priests would use to wash their hands and feet before performing ceremonies.

The tabernacle itself looked like an enormous tent. Its wooden framework was completely covered with gold. A linen drape embroidered with figures of angels formed the ceiling, and goatskin curtains covered the sides. Inside, the tabernacle was divided into two sections. The Holy of Holies held the golden Ark of the Covenant with its tablets of the Ten Commandments. The Holy Place, separated from the Holy of Holies by a linen curtain, contained a table, a golden altar on which to burn incense, and the great candlestick with seven branches.

When everything was in place, Moses blessed the people and thanked them for their work on the tabernacle. Then he turned to Aaron who stood near him and motioned to Aaron's four sons to join their father at his side. Solemnly he washed the hands and feet of Aaron and each of his sons in the copper basin. Next, he dressed Aaron in a long robe of checkered linen, linen trousers, a wide needle-point belt, and a linen turban. On his brother's head he placed a gold headpiece with the words HOLY TO THE LORD inscribed on it, and over Aaron's shoulders he dropped a heavy metal breastplate containing twelve precious stones —each standing for one of the twelve tribes of Israel. Silently, Moses dressed each of Aaron's sons in clothes similar to those of their father.

From this day forward, Moses told the people of Israel, Aaron and his sons would serve as the high priests of Israel. They would perform the people's sacrifices and carry the peoples' prayers to the Lord. They and the other members of the tribe of Levi would be responsible for guarding the tabernacle and carrying it from place to place as the Israelites moved along in their journeys.

Before all the congregation of Israel, Moses poured oil on Aaron's head, anointing him in the way kings and rulers of other lands were anointed. After that he slaughtered a bull that had been prepared as a sacrifice and placed it on the altar outside the tabernacle. Using both hands, he dipped into the blood of the bull and smeared drops of blood on the tip of Aaron's right ear, on the thumb of his right hand, and on the large toe of his right foot as a sign that his whole body was made holy to the Lord. Finally, Moses sprinkled blood and oil on the four gold horns of the altar, on Aaron, and on his sons to complete the ritual of their dedication as priests.

As the ceremonies drew to a close, the people saw a thick cloud move down from the sky to the top of the tabernacle. Glancing at Moses, they saw him kneel low and heard him praise "the glory of the Lord" which was hovering now over their sacred tabernacle. All together, the people knelt too, hiding their eyes from the strange and holy cloud.

In days to come that cloud became a guide to Moses and the people in their travels. When Moses saw the cloud resting over the tabernacle, he commanded the congregation to rest where they were. When the cloud seemed to lift away from the tabernacle, Moses and the Israelites moved on, folding the tabernacle like a tent, and following the cloud to their next camping place.

CHAPTER XXI

REVOLT IN THE DESERT

A trumpet blasted loudly through the morning air, awakening the Israelites with a start. Moses was calling to them on the silver trumpets that the artist Bezalel had made for him. One by one the people streamed from their tents and gathered in the courtyard outside the tabernacle, the official meeting place for the tribes of Israel. When everyone had assembled, Moses spoke.

The time had come for them to move on, he said. They had camped at Sinai for a year, and now they must gather their families and head for the promised land of Canaan. They would move in stages, one tribe after the other. The tribes of Judah, Issachar, and Zebulun would go first. Next would come Reuben, Simeon, and Gad, and after them Ephraim, Manasseh, and Benjamin. The tribes of Dan, Asher, and Naphtali would bring up the rear. At the head of the whole company would march the priests—the Levites—no longer counted as a tribe, but as servants of the Lord. They would carry the Ark of the Covenant and the sacred objects from the tabernacle.

With much excitement, the people of Israel packed their belongings and organized themselves into long columns behind the heads of their tribes. At a blast of the trumpet, they began their procession out of the desert of Sinai, the land of the Ten Commandments.

No sooner had the journey begun, than the old grumblings started. A short distance out of the Sinai wilderness, complaints that had been partly forgotten burst forth. The people wanted meat and fish to eat and comfortable houses in which to live. They wanted green fertile lands to till and an end to wandering in the desolate desert.

Loudest among the complainers was a man named Korah, the son of Izhar, a Levite. A big heavy man with thick lips and small eyes, Korah had opposed Moses from the beginning. He had always been jealous of Moses' influence on the people and his closeness to the God of Israel. But ever since Moses had appointed Aaron instead of Korah as high priest in Israel, Korah did not even try to hide his hatred and bitterness. He went from tribe to tribe speaking against Aaron and Moses and convincing the people that they should never have left Egypt.

Korah had three supporters, all from the tribe of Reuben. They were the brothers Dathan and Abiram, the sons of Eliab, and On, the son of Peleth. Like many others in the tribe of Reuben, these men felt that they and their tribesmen did not receive enough respect from Moses and the other tribes of Israel. Reuben had been the eldest son of Jacob, the father of the twelve tribes. As such, the Reubenites believed, Reuben's descendants should have special privileges. But Moses never treated them in any special way. If anything, he seemed to favor the tribe of Judah, just the way Jacob himself had favored his younger son Judah over his elder son Reuben. Even on their march from Sinai, Moses had sent the tribe of Judah first, when by right, the Reubenites insisted, they should have led the way.

Always malcontents, always unhappy, Korah, Dathan, Abiram, and On went among the people spreading rumors and pointing out the hardships ahead. On good days, when the journey went well, they did not get much support from the people. On bad days, however, outbursts would spread like brushfires, lighting discontent even among Moses' loyal supporters.

In the midst of the mumbling and grumbling, Moses remained calm. With a word here, a smile there, he somehow managed to control the bitterness and unhappiness that was breeding within the Israelite camp. He had to. He had much more important things to think about.

They were heading toward the wilderness of Paran, not far from the southern tip of Canaan. With their own strength and God's help, Moses believed, the Israelites could storm Canaan from the south and take over the lands that the Lord had promised them. But first he must know more about those lands. And to this end he had developed a plan.

One evening, he and Joshua went through the names of all the tribal leaders of Israel. From each tribe they chose a man who was noted for his strength and leadership. When they had checked off twelve names, they summoned the men to Moses' tent. Joshua himself had been chosen to represent the tribe of Ephraim.

With their approval, Moses told the men, he wanted them to go out and spy in the land of Canaan. It would be a dangerous mission, but essential to the Israelites.

"See what the land is," Moses instructed the spies, "and whether the people who dwell in it are strong or weak, whether they are few or many, and whether the land that they dwell in is good or bad, and whether the cities that they dwell in are camps or strongholds."

Without hesitation, the men accepted Moses' assignment. They would leave immediately and would travel at night, hiding by day from enemy eyes.

"Be of good courage," Moses bade them as he blessed each man. "And bring some of the fruit of the land," he called after them as they took leave of him.

If the spies brought back a good report, he would move quickly, leading the people directly into the Negev, the southern tip of Canaan. From there they would push their way upward until they had taken possession of the entire land.

Six weeks passed before Moses saw his spies again. Then one day, two ragged, wan-looking men entered the Israelite camp. Between them they carried a long pole, and from it hung huge clusters of juicy blue grapes. Behind them straggled other men, some carrying bright orange pomegranates, others carrying figs and dates.

Within minutes, word spread throughout the Israelite camp that the spies were home, and people rushed from all corners to greet their tribesmen. Without stopping to rest or wash up, the spies began their report.

They had split up into small groups shortly after leaving the Israelite camp, they explained. Each group had traveled to a different region of Canaan, and among them they had covered the whole land. They had explored the Negev in the south, Jericho and the Salt Sea district in the east, and the large cities of central Canaan—Jerusalem, Hebron, Schechem, Megiddo, Kadesh. They had joined forces again at Hebron, the region closest to the Israelite camp, and made their way back together. They had moved cautiously, hiding when they could or disguising themselves as inhabitants of the land.

Turning to Moses, one of the spies spoke slowly, choosing his words carefully.

"We came to the land to which you sent us," he said. "It flows with milk and honey, and this is its fruit."

A loud cheer went up as the people looked hungrily at the grapes, the pomegranates, and the figs.

"Yet the people who dwell in the land are strong," the spy continued, "and the cities are fortified and very large."

The cheers stopped and the people listened intently.

"The Amalekites dwell in the land of the Negev; the Hittites, the Jebusites, and the Amorites dwell in the hill country; and the Canaanites dwell by the sea, and along the Jordan."

A silence as thick as a wall hung over the camp.

"Let us go up at once, and occupy it," one of the spies shouted into the silence. Moses recognized him as Caleb the son of Jephunneh from the tribe of Judah, "for we are well able to overcome it."

Suddenly everybody began speaking at once.

"We are not able to go up against the people," one of the spies called out, "for they are stronger than we."

"The land, through which we have gone, to spy it out," interrupted another, "is a land that devours its inhabitants; and all the people that we saw in it are men of great stature."

"And we seemed to ourselves like grasshoppers," joined in still another, "and so we seemed to them."

By now the whole camp was clamoring. Men shouted and shook their fists, women screamed and cried. One after the other the curses, the shouts, the threats poured out.

"Would that we had died in the land of Egypt! Or would that we had died in this wilderness! Why does the Lord bring us into this land, to fall by the sword? Our wives and our little ones will become a prey; would it not be better for us to go back to Egypt?"

In the midst of the crowd, Moses could see Korah. The Reubenite's eyes were narrow and glinting, his voice coarse and rough, as he urged the people on in their anger.

Then over the cries of the people, Moses heard the clear, calm voice of Joshua.

"The land, which we passed through to spy it out, is an exceedingly good land," the young man said. "If the Lord delights in us, he will bring us into this land and give it to us, a land which flows with milk and honey. Only, do not rebel against the Lord; and do not fear the people of the land, for they are bread for us. . . . Do not fear them."

It was a good speech, but nobody paid attention. The other spies had frightened the people and convinced them that they would never succeed in overtaking the land. Nothing Moses or Joshua could say would help now. In angry groups, the people returned to their tents, turning from time to time to glower at Moses or to shout loudly that they needed to have a new leader.

During the next few weeks feelings ran high in the Israelite camp. Joshua did not allow Moses to step out of his tent alone, for fear somebody would attack him. All talk of an invasion of Canaan was dropped. Moses ordered the people to remain in the wilderness—indefinitely.

One morning, the anger that had been building for weeks burst loose. Korah, Dathan, and Abiram appeared at Moses' tent, along with two hundred and fifty Israelites, many of them Levites and Reubenites. They had fearsome demands to make: Moses must resign as leader of the Israelites. The people must return to Egypt at once. Aaron must be dismissed as high priest.

Korah served as spokesman.

"You have gone too far!" he shouted at Moses. "For all the congregation are holy, every one of them, and the

Lord is among them." He was sarcastically echoing words Moses had used many times. "Why then do you exalt yourselves above the assembly of the Lord?"

As though on cue, Dathan and Abiram added their insults.

"Is it a small thing that you have brought us up out of a land flowing with milk and honey, to kill us in the wilderness, that you must also make yourself a prince over us?" Dathan began. And Abiram completed his thought:

"Moreover you have not brought us into a land flowing with milk and honey, nor given us inheritance of fields and vineyards."

After more jibes, the rebels marched out, leaving Moses stunned and shaken. Calling Aaron and Joshua to his side, the old leader headed toward the holy tabernacle to pray for help.

As the men approached, they saw hundreds of Israelites milling around. In the midst of the crowd stood Korah, Dathan, and Abiram, receiving the compliments and applause of the people.

For a moment, Moses said nothing. Slowly he raised his eyes toward heaven and whispered words no man could hear. A second later he turned toward the mob, who had seen him by now and had begun taunting and jeering him.

With a voice controlled only by the greatest effort, he commanded the people:

"Depart, I pray you, from . . . these wicked men, and touch nothing of theirs, lest you be swept away with all their sins."

Frightened in spite of themselves, most of the Israelites moved away from the rebel leaders, leaving Dathan, Abiram, and Korah standing with their closest followers. Quickly, Moses spoke again:

"Hereby you shall know that the Lord has sent me to do all these works, and that it has not been of my own accord. If these men die the common death of all men, or if they are visited by the fate of all men, then the Lord has not sent me. But if the Lord creates something new, and the ground opens its mouth, and swallows them up, with all that belongs to them . . . then you shall know that these men have despised the Lord."

Before the last words were out of his mouth, an ear-shattering crack filled the air. As the people watched in horror, the earth around the rebel leaders split wide open, swallowing up Dathan, Abiram, and Korah. Almost at the same instant, flames shot forth from the ground, sweeping up all who had supported the rebels.

Screaming with terror, the Israelites fled to their tents, hiding helplessly from the wrath of Moses and his God.

Moses, too, returned to his quarters. Never before, even after the outrage of the golden calf, had he felt such fury —and such pain. Of all the things that had taken place during the last few weeks, one truth stood out clearly. These people, this generation of Israelites, would never be ready to enter Canaan, to build a new land and a new nation. For all his teaching, they remained slaves in their thinking, easily discouraged and taken in by every false promise. Their children might deserve the new land, but they themselves did not have the faith and the courage for it

And he? Moses himself? Somehow he suspected that he, too—with his impatience and his anger—he, too, was not worthy of entering the Promised Land.

CHAPTER XXII

No Man Knows the Place of His Burial

Life in the desert takes on a rhythm all its own. As far as the eye can see, vast stretches of barren land seem to roll and sway under the beat of a burning sun. Gentle winds blow constantly, moving the air but bringing little relief from the heavy heat of the wilderness. In the fall, the winds suddenly pick up force and become whirling sandstorms that blind and choke man and beast. In the winter, the sandstorms die down, the air becomes a little fresher, and warm days turn quickly into icy nights.

For Moses and the people of Israel, the rhythm of the desert marked the rhythm of their lives. Fall became winter, winter turned into summer, and another year passed. Another and another went by and still the people wandered in the desert. They lived the lives of nomads, carrying their belongings from place to place, seeking grasslands, food, and water.

Etzion-Gever, Kadesh-barnea, Mount Hor, Tzalmonath, Punon, Oroth. . . . Thousands of years later scholars would search out these place names mentioned in the Bible, would search the desert without success for traces of the wandering Hebrews of early days.

There were no traces to be found. For forty years the Children of Israel moved from oasis to oasis, living out their lives but leaving behind no mark that blowing sands and burning sun could not cover up forever.

As the years went by, the older generation of Israelites gradually died out. Those who had been born slaves in Egypt died free men in lands that belonged to no man. Their children, reared in freedom, took their places as tribal leaders, as herdsmen, as warriors.

It was as Moses had planned it.

"And your children shall be shepherds in the wilderness forty years," God had told Moses years ago after the spies and rebels had shaken the people's faith, ". . . until the last of your dead bodies lies in the wilderness. According to the number of days in which you spied out the land, forty days, for every day a year."

Now forty years had gone by, and Moses himself had become an old old man. Miraculously, he could still see and hear clearly and move about easily. But he could feel his age. He could feel it in his body and his mind—and in the loneliness that always surrounded him.

He was one hundred and twenty years old. He had lost

all those persons dearest to him. Long ago, his beloved wife Zipporah, the Midianite shepherdess, had died. Later, he had buried his sister Miriam at Kadesh-barnea. Most recently, his brother Aaron, his helper from the start, had died and been buried on Mount Hor.

Moses was the last of the old ones, the last of a world that no longer existed. When he was a young man, the Egyptians were the most powerful people in the world, the Assyrians and the Hittites their most feared enemies. Now Egyptian power was declining and the Hittite Empire all but vanished from the earth. Other nations had taken their place as world powers. From caravans that stopped to barter with the Israelites, Moses learned that the Philistines, or Sea Peoples, had grown large and powerful. These people were moving from the west into the land of Canaan, just as the Israelites were moving in from the east. Someday, Moses saw, that land would become a battleground between Philistines and Israelites. Someday the Israelites would rule the land, but they would have to fight, again and again, to hold onto it.

Someday was far in the future, and Moses was not part of that future. He would not be there to see the battles, to stir the people by lifting his arms high toward the sky.

Even now, he barely took part in the Israelite wars.

During the past two years, he had brought his people close to the land of Canaan. They had moved toward the eastern bank of the Jordan River, through lands occupied by the nations of Moab, Edom, and Ammon. Joshua, not Moses, had led the Israelites in fighting these peoples, who would not allow the Hebrews to cross their lands. Joshua, not Moses, had commanded the attacks and won victories over these enemy nations.

Moses could hardly get used to the weapons the people used. Swords and shields were made of a new metal, iron. The Egyptians had known of the metal even during Moses' youth, but the Hittites had first learned to mine it and turn it into weapons and tools. Through them, other peoples of the East had discovered its uses.

It was a new world and Joshua and his men were a new generation, a new breed of Israelites. Oh, they complained as their fathers had and, like their fathers, they cried out for food and water. But the men of this new generation were tough. They believed in themselves, in their leaders, and in their God.

They looked on Moses as a prophet. They brought their children to his tent to see him, a man of God with flowing white hair and long white beard. They came themselves on holy days and special occasions to pay their respects and receive his blessings. But he was not of them. They did not need him to guide their every step, to make every law and decision as he had once done.

His laws were written on scrolls now. The priests served as scribes, copying old scrolls Moses gave them and making corrections and changes as they arose. There were dozens of judges now, too, lower judges and higher judges carefully organized into a system that Moses had worked out.

He could look back with satisfaction on all he had accomplished. He had prepared the people well. They were ready to enter the Promised Land he had spoken about to them so often. They were ready. He was not. He had always known he would not enter that land he loved more than any place on earth. He had known it in his heart and he had heard it from his God. He, too, had been weak at times. He, too, had grown bitter and impatient. He belonged to that other generation, the old ones, the generation of the wanderers. He could see the land, but it would not be his to live in.

Long ago he had put things in order for his final hours. He had chosen Joshua to succeed him as leader of the Israelites. "Be strong and of good courage," he had instructed Joshua, "for you shall go with this people into the land which the Lord has sworn to their fathers to give them. . . . Do not fear or be dismayed."

He had taught Joshua the rules and regulations, the ceremonies and beliefs which the people of Israel were to practice in their homeland. He had even shown Joshua how to behave after his death. When the time came for Moses to depart this earth, he told his assistant, no man was to know his burial place. In Egypt, people worshiped the tombs of their kings, as though the kings were gods and their tombs were sacred. Israel had one God and they had been taught to worship Him by obeying His commandments. Moses did not want his grave to become a holy place, to confuse the people into thinking he was a god.

The time Moses spoke about to Joshua had now come. Every day the Israelites drew closer to their land. Some of the tribes—Reuben, Gad, and half the tribe of Manasseh—had already settled in territories they had conquered east of the Jordan. The others were ready to take possession of the lands west of the Jordan.

The time had come. Moses knew it. He knew it from the moment he awoke this morning. He knew it by the feeling of excitement and expectation he had. He knew it by the—Was it fear he felt, fear at leaving the world of the known for the mysteries of the unknown?

During the morning, Moses went through the camp,

moving from one tribal group to another. For each tribe he had a blessing.

> *Let Reuben live, and not die,*
> *nor let his men be few.* . . .
> *Hear, O Lord, the voice of Judah,*
> *and bring him in to his people.* . . .
> *Rejoice, Zebulun, in your going out;*
> *and Issachar, in your tents.* . . .

To each tribe, he had something to say. He walked erect, his head high, his eyes shining that special light the people had seen many times before.

In the afternoon, he assembled all the people. He stood before them, a familiar figure, and still somehow unfamiliar. He stood as though between heaven and earth and spoke to them about the past, the present, and the future. With a voice that had lost none of its force, he called out to them a song he had written.

> *Give ear, O heavens, and I will speak;*
> *and let the earth hear the words of my mouth.*
> *May my teaching drop as the rain,*
> *my speech distil as the dew,*
> *as the gentle rain upon the tender grass,*
> *and as the showers upon the herb.*

For I will proclaim the name of the Lord.
Ascribe greatness to our God!

Louder and louder Moses' song became. Some of the words were tender and loving:

> *. . . For the Lord's portion is his people,*
> *Jacob his allotted heritage.*
> *He found him in a desert land, and in the*
> *howling waste of the wilderness;*
> *he encircled him, he cared for him,*
> *he kept him as the apple of his eye. . . .*

Other parts of Moses' song were stern and threatening, a warning to the people should they stray from the Lord:

"And I will heap evils upon them;
I will spend my arrows upon them;
they shall be wasted with hunger, and
devoured with burning heat and poisonous pestilence;
and I will send the teeth of beasts against them,
with venom of crawling things of the dust. . . ."

When he had finished his song, Moses turned from the people gathered before him and walked slowly away. The afternoon was drawing to a close and the hills and mountains around the camp cast long shadows over the

Israelite tents. Without moving and without speaking, the people watched as Moses walked toward one of the mountains, Mount Nebo, and slowly disappeared in the distance as dusk, then darkness covered the Israelite camp.

Moses never returned from that mountain. He died there quietly, at the top of the mountain, overlooking the land he had longed for but could never know. And to this day, no man knows the place of his burial.

And there has not arisen a prophet since in Israel like Moses, whom the Lord knew face to face, none like him for all the signs and the wonders which the Lord sent him to do in the land of Egypt, to Pharaoh and to all his servants and to all his land, and for all the mighty power and all the great and terrible deeds which Moses wrought in the sight of all Israel.

Deuteronomy 34:10-12

THE TEN COMMANDMENTS

An Appendix

Of all the commandments Moses gave the people of Israel, the Ten Commandments have been regarded through the ages as among the most sacred laws of the Bible. They appear in the Bible in the Book of Exodus, Chapter 20, and again, with some variations, in the Book of Deuteronomy, Chapter 5.

The Protestant, Roman Catholic, and Jewish religions all accept these commandments as basic to the teachings of their faiths. Each of these religions, however, numbers the commandments a little differently. Roman Catholics combine the first two commandments of the Protestant version of the Bible and regard these as the first commandment. They divide the last commandment into two, to form ten. Jews regard the words, "I am the Lord thy God who brought thee out of the land of Egypt, out of the house of bondage," as the entire first commandment. Protestants consider these words a preface to the actual commandments, and Roman Catholics incorporate them into their longer first commandment. The

Jewish Bible also combines the first two commandments of the Protestant Bible and considers this the second commandment.

Protestant, Roman Catholic, and Jewish versions of the Ten Commandments are given on the following pages. Each version follows a translation of the Bible accepted by that religious group. For the Protestant version, the King James translation of the Bible is used. The Ten Commandments according to the Revised Standard translation appear in this book in Chapter 16, "At the Foot of the Mountain."

Protestant Version According to the King James Translation

I.   Thou shalt have no other gods before me.

II.   Thou shalt not make unto thee any graven image, or any likeness of any thing that is in heaven above, or that is in the earth beneath, or that is in the water under the earth: Thou shalt not bow down thyself to them, nor serve them for I the Lord thy God am a jealous God, visiting the iniquity of the fathers upon the children unto the third and fourth generations of them that hate me; and shewing mercy unto thousands of them that love me and keep my commandments.

III.   Thou shalt not take the name of the Lord thy God in vain; for the Lord will not hold him guiltless that taketh his name in vain.

IV.   Remember the sabbath day, to keep it holy. Six days shalt thou labor, and do all thy work: But the seventh day is the sabbath of the Lord thy God: in it thou shalt not do any work, thou, nor thy son, nor thy daughter, thy man-servant, nor thy maidservant, nor thy cattle, nor thy stranger that is within thy gates: For in six days the Lord made heaven and earth, the sea, and all that in them is, and rested the

163

seventh day: wherefore the Lord blessed the sabbath day, and hallowed it.

V.   Honour thy father and thy mother: that thy days may be long upon the land which the Lord thy God giveth thee.

VI.   Thou shalt not kill.

VII.   Thou shalt not commit adultery.

VIII.   Thou shalt not steal.

IX.   Thou shalt not bear false witness against thy neighbour.

X.   Thou shalt not covet thy neighbour's house, thou shalt not covet thy neighbour's wife, nor his manservant, nor his maidservant, nor his ox, nor his ass, nor any thing that is thy neighbour's.

Roman Catholic Version According to the Douay Translation

I. I am the Lord thy God, thou shalt not have strange
gods before me. Thou shalt not make to thyself a graven
thing, nor the likeness of any thing that is in heaven above,
or in the earth beneath, nor of those things that are in the
waters under the earth. Thou shalt not adore them, nor serve
them: I am the Lord thy God, mighty, jealous, visiting the
iniquity of the fathers upon the children, unto the third and
fourth generation of them that hate me: And shewing mercy
unto thousands of them that love me, and keep my commandments.

II. Thou shalt not take the name of the Lord thy God
in vain: for the Lord will not hold him guiltless that shall
take the name of the Lord his God in vain.

III. Remember that thou keep holy the sabbath day. Six
days shalt thou labour, and shalt do all thy works. But on the
seventh day is the sabbath of the Lord thy God: thou shalt do
no work on it, thou nor thy son, nor thy daughter, nor thy
manservant, nor thy maidservant, nor they beast, nor the
stranger that is within thy gates. For in six days the Lord

made heaven and earth, and the sea, and all things that are in them, and rested on the seventh day: therefore the Lord blessed the seventh day, and sanctified it.

IV.   Honour thy father and thy mother, that thou mayest be longlived upon the land which the Lord thy God will give thee.

V.   Thou shalt not kill.

VI.   Thou shalt not commit adultery.

VII.   Thou shalt not steal.

VIII.   Thou shalt not bear false witness against thy neighbour.

IX.   Thou shalt not covet thy neighbour's wife.

*X.   Nor his house, nor his field, nor his manservant, nor his maidservant, nor his ox, nor his ass, nor any thing that is his.

* In the Catechism the last commandment is simply, "Thou shalt not covet thy neighbour's goods."

*Jewish Version According to the Masoretic Text, Translation
of the Jewish Publication Society of America*

I.   I am the Lord thy God, who brought thee out of the
land of Egypt, out of the house of bondage.

II.   Thou shalt have no other gods before me. Thou shalt
not make unto thee a graven image, nor any manner of likeness, of anything that is in heaven above, or that is in the
earth beneath, or that is in the water under the earth; thou
shalt not bow down unto them, nor serve them; for I the Lord
thy God am a jealous God, visiting the iniquity of the fathers
upon the children unto the third and fourth generation of
them that hate me; and showing mercy unto the thousandth
generation of them that love me and keep my commandments.

III.   Thou shalt not take the name of the Lord thy God
in vain; for the Lord will not hold him guiltless that taketh
His name in vain.

IV.   Remember the sabbath day, to keep it holy. Six days
shalt thou labour, and do all thy work; but the seventh day
is a sabbath unto the Lord thy God, in it thou shalt not do any
manner of work, thou, nor thy son, nor thy daughter, nor

thy man-servant, nor thy maid-servant, nor thy cattle, nor thy stranger that is within thy gates.

V.   Honour thy father and thy mother, that thy days may be long upon the land which the Lord thy God giveth thee.

VI.   Thou shalt not murder.

VII.   Thou shalt not commit adultery.

VIII.   Thou shalt not steal.

IX.   Thou shalt not bear false witness against thy neighbour.

X.   Thou shalt not covet thy neighbour's house; thou shalt not covet thy neighbour's wife, nor his man-servant, nor his maid-servant, nor his ox, nor his ass, nor any thing that is thy neighbour's.

INDEX

Aaron, 14, 45–69, 77, 91, 98–
    102, 116–123, 133, 137,
    138, 141, 148, 153
Abihu, 47
Abiram, 141, 148, 149
Abraham, 4, 6, 7
Ahisamach, 134
Amalekites, 145; battle with,
    96–102
Amenhotep IV, 131
Ammon, 154
Amorites, 39, 145
Amram, 14
Aqaba, Gulf of, 81
Ark of the Covenant, 136–140
Assyrians, 9, 128

Bezalel, 134–136
Burning bush revelation, 37–45

Caleb, 145
Canaan, 4, 5, 39, 80, 81, 114,
    140, 142–144, 147, 153,
    154

Canaanites, 145
Children of Israel, 4–7, 89, 102,
    104, 152

Dathan, 141, 142, 148, 149

Edom, 154
Eleazar, 47
Eliab, 141, 142
Eliezer, 46
Elim, oasis of, 93
Elisheba, 47
Exodus, the, 78–123, 133–159

Gershom, 35, 46
Gizeh, 22
Gods of Egypt, 20, 21, 42
Goshen, 6, 10, 25, 27, 49, 54,
    64–66, 73, 75

Hammurabi, laws of, 129, 130
Hebron, 144

169